Coaching Youth Wrestling

THIRD EDITION

American Sport Education Program

Human Kinetics

Library of Congress Cataloging-in-Publication Data

Coaching youth wrestling / American Sport Education Program. -- 3rd ed.
    p. cm.
  ISBN-13: 978-0-7360-6711-9 (soft cover)
  ISBN-10: 0-7360-6711-6 (soft cover)
  1. Wrestling for children--Coaching--United States--Handbooks, manuals, etc.
I. American Sport Education Program.
  GV1196.3.C63 2008
  796.812--dc22   2007024462

  ISBN-10: 0-7360-6711-6
  ISBN-13: 978-0-7360-6711-9

Acquisitions Editors: Emma Sandberg and Nathan T. Bell; **Project Writers:** USA Wrestling Staff; **Project Consultant:** Pete Sandberg; **Developmental Editor:** Laura Floch; **Assistant Editor:** Cory Weber; **Copyeditor:** Annette Pierce; **Proofreader:** Julie Marx Goodreau; **Permission Manager:** Carly Breeding; **Graphic Designer:** Nancy Rasmus; **Graphic Artists:** Sandra Meier and Kim McFarland; **Cover Designer:** Keith Blomberg; **Photographer (cover):** Sport the Library; **Photographer (interior):** Tim De Frisco; photos on pages 1, 9, 19, 33, 48, 51, 57, 69, 81, 111, 149, and 161 courtesy of John Sachs and Tony Rotundo/Tech-Fall.com; **Photo Asset Manager:** Laura Fitch; **Visual Production Assistant:** Joyce Brumfield; **Photo Office Assistant:** Jason Allen; **Art Manager:** Kelly Hendren; **Illustrator:** Alan L. Wilborn; **Printer:** United Graphics

We thank USA Wrestling in Colorado Springs, CO, for assistance in providing the location for the photo shoot for this book.

Copies of this book are available at special discounts for bulk purchase for sales promotions, premiums, fund-raising, or educational use. Special editions or book excerpts can also be created to specifications. For details, contact the Special Sales Manager at Human Kinetics.

Printed in the United States of America   10   9   8   7   6   5   4   3   2

Human Kinetics
Web site: www.HumanKinetics.com

United States: Human Kinetics
P.O. Box 5076, Champaign, IL 61825-5076
800-747-4457
e-mail: humank@hkusa.com

Canada: Human Kinetics
475 Devonshire Road Unit 100
Windsor, ON N8Y 2L5
800-465-7301 (in Canada only)
e-mail: orders@hkcanada.com

Europe: Human Kinetics
107 Bradford Road, Stanningley
Leeds LS28 6AT, United Kingdom
+44 (0) 113 255 5665
e-mail: hk@hkeurope.com

Australia: Human Kinetics
57A Price Avenue
Lower Mitcham, South Australia 5062
08 8277 1555
e-mail: info@hkaustralia.com

New Zealand: Human Kinetics
Division of Sports Distributors NZ Ltd.
P.O. Box 300 226 Albany
North Shore City, Auckland
0064 9 448 1207
e-mail: info@humankinetics.co.nz

Contents

Welcome to Coaching iv

Welcome From USA Wrestling v

1   Stepping Into Coaching 1

2   Communicating as a Coach 9

3   Understanding Rules and Equipment 19

4   Providing for Wrestlers' Safety 33

5   Making Practices Fun and Practical 51

6   Teaching and Shaping Skills 57

7   Developing the Seven Basic Skills 69

8   Coaching Attacks and Counterattacks 81

9   Coaching Top and Bottom Techniques 111

10   Coaching Competitions 149

11   Developing Season and Practice Plans 161

Appendix A: Related Checklists and Forms 175

Appendix B: Wrestling Terms 181

Appendix C: 23 Wrestling Activities 185

About ASEP 199

Welcome to Coaching

Coaching young people is an exciting way to be involved in sport. But it isn't easy. Some coaches are overwhelmed by the responsibilities involved in helping athletes through their early sport experiences. And that's not surprising, because coaching youngsters requires more than telling them to lace up their shoes and step on the mat. It also involves preparing athletes physically and mentally to compete effectively, fairly, and safely in their sport, as well as providing them with a positive role model.

This book will help you meet the challenges and experience the many rewards of coaching young wrestlers. You'll learn how to meet your responsibilities as a coach, how to communicate well and provide for safety, and how to teach wrestling skills while keeping them fun. You'll also learn strategies for coaching on match day. To help you with your practices, more than 23 wrestling activities are included throughout the text and in one of the book's appendixes. We also provide sample practice plans and season plans to help guide you throughout your season.

This book serves as a text for ASEP's Coaching Youth Wrestling course. If you would like more information about this course or other American Sport Education Program courses and resources, please contact us at the following address:

ASEP
P.O. Box 5076
Champaign, IL 61825-5076
800-747-5698
www.ASEP.com

Welcome From USA Wrestling

Whether you are a volunteer club coach or a scholastic coach with a little experience, you already know that youngsters are not mature adults. Young people have different perspectives, experience different emotions, and set different goals than older people do. They present special challenges to a coach because they react differently than adults do to instruction, criticism, encouragement, failure, and success. This book, which is intended for adults with little or no formal preparation for coaching wrestlers, will help you meet those challenges and experience the rewards of coaching young athletes.

Coaching Youth Wrestling is the result of a joint effort by USA Wrestling and the American Sport Education Program (ASEP). The book serves as the Copper-level text in USA Wrestling's National Coaches Education Program (NCEP). It is the first resource wrestling coaches need to advance to Bronze, Silver, and Gold levels of certification in NCEP.

USA Wrestling and ASEP hope you will find coaching rewarding and will continue to learn more about coaching and the sport of wrestling so that you can be the best possible coach for your athletes. Good coaching!

For more information about this coaching education program, please contact the following:

USA Wrestling
National Coaches Education Program
6155 Lehman Drive
Colorado Springs, CO 80918
719-598-8181

Stepping Into Coaching

I f you are like most youth wrestling coaches, you have probably been recruited from the ranks of involved parents, sport enthusiasts, or community volunteers. Like many rookie and veteran coaches, you probably have had little formal instruction on how to coach. But when the call went out for coaches to assist with the local youth wrestling program, you answered because you like children and enjoy wrestling, and perhaps because you want to be involved in a worthwhile community activity.

Your initial coaching assignment may be difficult. Like many volunteers, you may not know everything there is to know about wrestling or about how to work with children. *Coaching Youth Wrestling* presents the basics of coaching wrestling. To start, we look at your responsibilities and what's involved in being a coach. We also talk about what to do when your own child is on the team you coach, and we examine five tools for being an effective coach.

Your Responsibilities as a Coach

Coaching wrestling at all levels involves more than just technique and practice on the mat. Coaching involves accepting the tremendous responsibility you face when parents put their children into your care. Liability issues, first aid, and even hygiene can fall into the realm of a coach's duties. As a wrestling coach, you'll be called on to do the following:

1. *Provide a safe physical environment.*

   As a coach you're responsible for regularly inspecting the practice and competition areas and equipment (see "Facilities and Equipment Checklist" in appendix A on page 176).

2. *Communicate in a positive way.*

   As you might have already guessed, you will have a lot to communicate. You'll communicate not only with your wrestlers and their parents but also with the coaching staff, officials, administrators, and others. Communicate in a way that is positive and that demonstrates that you have the best interests of the athletes at heart (see chapter 2 for more information).

3. *Teach the fundamental skills of wrestling.*

   When teaching the fundamental skills of wrestling, remember that you want your wrestlers to have fun. Help all wrestlers become the best they can be by creating a fun, yet productive, practice environment by taking a *games approach* to teaching and practicing skills, an approach that kids thoroughly enjoy (see chapter 5 for more information). Additionally, to help your wrestlers improve their skills, you need a sound understanding of wrestling skills (see chapters 7 through 9).

Coaching Tip

Set a goal for yourself to make at least two positive comments to each athlete during each practice.

4. *Teach the rules of wrestling.*

   Introduce the rules of wrestling and incorporate them into individual instruction (see chapter 3 for more information). Because wrestling does not appear on television as often as other sports, most athletes will have very little background knowledge in the basic rules of the sport. Referencing the rules in practice will help athletes learn the makeup of a wrestling match. Simple concepts such as "shoulders breaking a 45-degree plane for near fall" are rules that kids won't know ahead of time. Review the rules anytime an opportunity naturally arises in practices.

5. *Direct wrestlers in competition.*

   Your responsibilities include assigning wrestlers to each weight group, relating appropriately to officials and to opposing coaches and wrestlers, and making sound tactical decisions during matches (see chapter 10 for more information on coaching during competitions). Remember that the focus is not on winning at all costs, but on coaching your kids to compete well, do their best, improve their wrestling skills, and strive to win within the rules.

6. *Help your wrestlers become fit and value fitness for a lifetime.*

   To wrestle safely and successfully, wrestlers need to be fit. Help your wrestlers learn to become fit on their own, understand the value of fitness, and enjoy training. To that end, do not make athletes do push-ups or run laps for punishment. Make it fun to get fit for wrestling, and make it fun to wrestle so that your wrestlers will want to stay fit for a lifetime.

7. *Help young people develop character.*

   Character development includes learning, caring, being honest and respectful, and taking responsibility. Helping athletes develop these qualities is no less important than teaching them the skill of cradling for a pin. Teach these characteristics by demonstrating and encouraging behaviors that express them. For example, a tough practice consisting of conditioning and hard wrestling may naturally lead you to talk about the value of hard work, commitment, and the desire to accomplish a lofty goal.

Coaching Your Own Child

Coaching can become even more complicated when your child wrestles on the team you coach. Many coaches are parents, but the two roles should not be confused. As a parent, you are responsible only for yourself and your child, but as a coach, you are also responsible for the organization, all the wrestlers on the team, and their parents. Because of this additional responsibility, your behavior on the wrestling mat will be different from your behavior at home, and your son or daughter may not understand why.

For example, imagine the confusion of a young boy who is the center of his parents' attention at home but is barely noticed by his father (who is the coach) in the sport setting. Or consider the mixed signals sent to a young girl when her mother, who usually comments infrequently on her activities, constantly evaluates her skills when acting as her coach.

Coaching Tip
When coaching your own child, do not discuss wrestling at home unless your child initiates the conversation.

Explain to your child your new responsibilities and how they will affect your relationship when coaching. Take the following steps to avoid problems in coaching your own child:

- Ask your child if he or she wants you to coach the team.
- Explain why you want to be involved with the team.
- Discuss with your child how your interactions will change when you take on the role of coach at practices or games.
- Limit your coaching behavior to when you are in the coaching role.
- Avoid parenting during practice or game situations to keep your role clear in your child's mind.
- Reaffirm your love for your child, irrespective of his or her performance on the wrestling mat.

Five Tools of an Effective Coach

Have you purchased the traditional coaching tools—things such as whistles, coaching clothes, wrestling shoes, and a clipboard? They'll help you in the act of coaching, but to be successful, you'll need five other tools that cannot be bought. These tools are available only through self-examination and hard work; they're easy to remember with the acronym COACH:

C   Comprehension

O   Outlook

A   Affection

C   Character

H   Humor

Comprehension

Comprehension of the rules and skills of wrestling is required. You must understand the elements of the sport. To improve your comprehension of wrestling, take the following steps:

- Read about the rules of wrestling in chapter 3 of this book.
- Read about the fundamental skills of wrestling in chapters 7 through 9 of this book.
- Read additional books on coaching wrestling.
- Contact youth wrestling organizations.
- Attend clinics on coaching wrestling.
- Talk with more experienced coaches.
- Observe local college, high school, and youth wrestling competitions.
- Watch wrestling on television.

In addition to having wrestling knowledge, you must also implement proper training and safety methods so that your wrestlers can participate with little risk of injury. Even then, injuries may occur. And more often than not, you'll be the first person responding to your athletes' injuries, so be sure you understand the basic emergency care procedures described in chapter 4. Also, read in that chapter how to handle more serious sport injury situations.

Outlook

This coaching tool refers to your perspective and goals—what you seek as a coach. The most common coaching objectives are to (a) have fun; (b) help wrestlers develop their physical, mental, and social skills; and (c) strive to win. Thus, your outlook involves your priorities, your planning, and your vision for the future. See "Assessing Your Priorities" to learn more about the priorities you set for yourself as a coach.

ASEP has a motto that will help you keep your outlook in line with the best interests of the kids on your team. It summarizes in four words all you need to remember when establishing your coaching priorities:

Athletes First, Winning Second

This motto recognizes that striving to win is an important, even vital, part of sports. But it emphatically states that no efforts in striving to win should be made at the expense of the athletes' well-being, development, and enjoyment. Take the following actions to better define your outlook:

- With the members of your coaching staff, determine your priorities for the season.
- Prepare for situations that may challenge your priorities.
- Set goals for yourself and your wrestlers that are consistent with your priorities.
- Plan how you and your wrestlers can best attain your goals.
- Review your goals frequently to be sure that you are staying on track.

Assessing Your Priorities

Even though all coaches focus on competition, we want you to focus on *positive* competition—keeping the pursuit of victory in perspective by making decisions that, first, are in the best interest of the wrestlers and, second, will help to win the match.

So, how do you know if your outlook and priorities are in order? Here's a little test:

1. Which situation would you be most proud of?
   a. *knowing that each participant enjoyed wrestling*
   b. *seeing that all athletes improved their wrestling skills*
   c. *winning the league championship*

2. Which statement best reflects your thoughts about sport?
   a. *If it isn't fun, don't do it.*
   b. *Everyone should learn something every day.*
   c. *Wrestling isn't fun if you don't win.*

3. How would you like your wrestlers to remember you?
   a. *as a coach who was fun to wrestle for*
   b. *as a coach who provided a good base of fundamental skills*
   c. *as a coach who had a winning record*

4. Which would you most like to hear a parent of a wrestler on your team say?
   a. *Mike really had a good time wrestling this year.*
   b. *Nicole learned some important lessons wrestling this year.*
   c. *Willie was on the championship wrestling team this year.*

5. Which of the following would be the most rewarding moment of your season?
   a. *having your team want to continue wrestling, even after practice is over*
   b. *seeing one of your wrestlers finally master a difficult upper-body throw*
   c. *winning the league championship*

Look over your answers. If you most often selected "a" responses, then having fun is most important to you. A majority of "b" answers suggests that skill development is what attracts you to coaching. And if "c" was your most frequent response, winning is tops on your list of coaching priorities. If your priorities are in order, your wrestlers' well-being will take precedence over your team's win–loss record every time.

Affection

Another vital tool you will want to have in your coaching kit is a genuine concern for the young people you coach. This requires having a passion for kids, a desire to share with them your enjoyment and knowledge of wrestling, and the patience and understanding that allow all your wrestlers to grow from their involvement in sport. You can demonstrate your affection and patience in many ways, including the following:

- Make an effort to get to know each wrestler on your team.
- Treat each wrestler as an individual.
- Empathize with wrestlers trying to learn new and difficult skills.
- Treat wrestlers as you would like to be treated under similar circumstances.
- Control your emotions.
- Show your enthusiasm for being involved with your team.
- Keep an upbeat tempo and positive tone in all of your communications.

Character

The fact that you have decided to coach young wrestlers probably means that you think participation in sport is important. But whether or not that participation develops character in your wrestlers depends as much on you as it does on the sport itself. How can you help your wrestlers build character?

Having good character means modeling appropriate behaviors for sport and life. That means more than just saying the right things. What you say and what you do must match. There is no place in coaching for the "Do as I say, not as I do" philosophy. Challenge, support, encourage, and reward every youngster, and your wrestlers will be more likely to accept each other, differences and all. Be in control before, during, and after all practices and competitions. And don't be afraid to admit that you were wrong. No one is perfect!

Each member of your coaching staff should consider the following steps to becoming a good role model:

- Take stock of your strengths and weaknesses.
- Build on your strengths.
- Set personal goals to improve areas where you are not as strong.
- If you slip up, apologize to your team and to yourself. You'll do better next time.

Humor

Humor is an often overlooked coaching tool. It means having the ability to laugh at yourself and with your wrestlers during practices and competitions. Nothing helps balance the seriousness of a skill session like a chuckle or two. And a sense of humor puts in perspective the many mistakes your wrestlers will make. So don't get upset over each miscue or respond negatively to erring wrestlers. Allow your wrestlers and yourself to enjoy the ups, and don't dwell on the downs. Here are some tips for injecting humor and fun into your practices:

- Make practices fun by including a variety of activities.
- Keep all wrestlers involved in games and skill practices.
- Consider laughter by your wrestlers to be a sign of enjoyment, not of waning discipline.
- Smile!

2

Communicating as a Coach

I n chapter 1, you learned about the tools you need for coaching: comprehension, outlook, affection, character, and humor. These are essentials for effective coaching; without them, you'd have a difficult time getting started. But none of the tools will work if you don't know how to use them with your wrestlers—and this requires skillful communication. This chapter examines what communication is and how you can become a more effective communicator.

Coaches often mistakenly believe that communication occurs only when instructing wrestlers to do something, but verbal commands are only a small part of the communication process. More than half of what is communicated is done so nonverbally. So remember this when you are coaching: Actions speak louder than words.

Communication in its simplest form involves two people: a sender and a receiver. The sender transmits the message verbally, through facial expressions, and possibly through body language. Once the message is sent, the receiver must receive it and, optimally, understand it. A receiver who fails to pay attention or listen will miss part, if not all, of the message.

Sending Effective Messages

Young wrestlers often have little understanding of the rules and skills of wrestling and probably even less confidence in their ability to wrestle. So they need accurate, understandable, and supportive messages to help them along. That's why your verbal and nonverbal messages are important.

Verbal Messages

"Sticks and stones may break my bones, but words will never hurt me" isn't true. Spoken words can have a strong and long-lasting effect. And coaches' words are particularly influential because youngsters place great importance on what coaches say. Like many former youth sport participants, you may have a difficult time remembering much of anything you were told by your elementary school teachers, but you can probably still recall several specific things your coaches at that level said to you. Such is the lasting effect of a coach's comments to an athlete.

Whether you are correcting misbehavior, teaching a wrestler how to counter a double leg, or praising a wrestler for good effort, you should consider several things when sending a message verbally:

- Be positive and honest.
- State it clearly and simply.
- Say it loud enough, and say it again.
- Be consistent.

Be Positive and Honest

Nothing turns people off like hearing someone nag all the time, and athletes react similarly to a coach who gripes constantly. Kids particularly need encouragement because they often doubt their ability to perform in a sport. So look for and tell your wrestlers what they did well.

But don't cover up poor or incorrect wrestling with rosy words of praise. Kids know all too well when they've erred, and no cheerfully expressed cliché can undo their mistakes. If you fail to acknowledge errors, your wrestlers will think you are a phony.

An effective way to correct a performance error is to first point out the part of the skill that the wrestler performed correctly. Then explain—in a positive manner—the error that the wrestler made and demonstrate the correct way to do it. Finish by encouraging the wrestler and emphasizing the correct performance.

Be sure not to follow a positive statement with the word *but*. For example, you shouldn't say, "Nice shot, Chris, but if you would keep your elbows in a little more, you'd get the takedown." This causes many kids to ignore the positive statement and focus on the negative one. Instead, you should say something like, "That was a good setup for your shot, Chris. And if you move your elbows in a little more, you'll get that takedown next time. That was right on target. Way to go."

State It Clearly and Simply

Positive and honest messages are good, but only if expressed directly in words your wrestlers understand. Beating around the bush is ineffective and inefficient. And if you ramble, your wrestlers will miss the point of your message and probably lose interest. Here are some tips for saying things clearly:

- Organize your thoughts before speaking to your wrestlers.
- Know your subject as completely as possible.
- Explain things thoroughly, but don't bore your wrestlers with long-winded monologues.
- Use language your wrestlers can understand, and be consistent in your terminology. Avoid trying to be hip by using their age group's slang.

Say It Loud Enough, and Say It Again

Talk to your team in a voice that all members can hear. A crisp, vigorous voice commands attention and respect; garbled and weak speech is tuned out. It's okay and, in fact, appropriate to soften your voice when speaking to a wrestler individually about a personal problem. But most of the time your messages will be for all your athletes to hear, so make sure they can. An enthusiastic voice also motivates wrestlers and tells them you enjoy being their coach. A word of caution, however: Avoid dominating the setting with a booming voice that distracts attention from wrestlers' performances.

Coaching Tip
Remember, terms that you are familiar with and understand may be completely foreign to your wrestlers, especially younger wrestlers or beginners. You may need to use demonstrations with your athletes so they can "see" the term and how it relates to the sport of wrestling.

Sometimes what you say, even if stated loudly and clearly, won't sink in the first time. This may be particularly true when young athletes hear words they don't understand. To avoid boring repetition and still get your message across, say the same thing in a slightly different way. For instance, you might first tell your wrestlers, "Remember to keep your feet wide when you're in your stance." If they don't appear to understand, you might say, "When you're wrestling on your feet, if you keep your feet spread apart, you'll be able to better defend against your opponent's attacks." The second form of the message may get through to wrestlers who missed it the first time around.

Be Consistent

People often say things in ways that imply a different message. For example, a touch of sarcasm added to the words "Way to go!" sends an entirely different message than the words themselves suggest. Avoid sending mixed messages. Keep the tone of your voice consistent with the words you use. And don't say something one day and contradict it the next; your wrestlers will get their wires crossed.

Keep your terminology consistent. Many wrestling terms describe the same or similar skills. One coach may use the term *post* when referring to the action that lifts a defender's arms out of the way on a shot, while another coach may call this a *pop*. Although both are correct, to be consistent as a staff, all coaches should agree on terms before the start of the season and then stay with them.

Nonverbal Messages

Just as you should match your tone of voice to the words you use, you should also match your nonverbal message to the verbal message. An extreme example of failing to do this would be shaking your head, indicating disapproval, while at the same time telling a wrestler "Nice try." Which is the wrestler to believe, your gesture or your words?

Messages can be sent nonverbally in several ways. Facial expressions and body language are just two of the more obvious forms of nonverbal signals that can help you when you coach. Keep in mind that as a coach you need to be a teacher first, so avoid any action that detracts from the message you are trying to convey.

Facial Expressions

The look on a person's face is the quickest clue to what the person thinks or feels. Your wrestlers know this, so they will study your face, looking for a sign that will tell them more than the words you say. Don't try to fool them by putting on a happy or blank mask. They'll see through it, and you'll lose credibility.

Serious, stone-faced expressions provide no cues to kids who want to know how they are performing. When faced with this, kids will just assume you're unhappy or disinterested. Don't be afraid to smile. A smile from a coach can give a great boost to an unsure wrestler. Plus, a smile lets your wrestlers know that you are happy coaching them. But don't overdo it, or your wrestlers won't be able to tell when you are genuinely pleased by something they've done or when you are just putting on a smiling face.

Body Language

What would your wrestlers think you were feeling if you came to practice slouched over, with your head down and your shoulders slumped? Would they think you were tired, bored, or unhappy? What would they think you were feeling if you watched them during a match with your hands on your hips, your jaws clenched, and your face reddened? Would they think you were upset with them, disgusted at an official, or mad at a fan? Probably some or all of these things would enter your wrestlers' minds. And none is the impression you want your wrestlers to have of you. That's why you should carry yourself in a pleasant, confident, and energetic manner.

Physical contact can also be an important use of body language. A handshake, a pat on the head, an arm around the shoulder, and even a big hug are effective ways to show approval, concern, affection, and joy to your wrestlers. Youngsters are especially in need of this type of nonverbal message. Keep within the obvious moral and legal limits, of course, but don't be reluctant to touch your wrestlers, sending a message that can only be expressed in that way.

> **Coaching Tip**
> As a coach, be aware of your body language. You must ensure that your wrestlers are translating it correctly and that you are providing a good example for your wrestlers to model.

Improving Your Receiving Skills

Now let's examine the other half of the communication process: receiving messages. Too often very good senders are very poor receivers of messages. But as a coach of young wrestlers, you must be able to fulfill both roles effectively.

The requirements for receiving messages are quite simple, but receiving skills are perhaps less satisfying and therefore underdeveloped compared to sending skills. People seem to enjoy hearing themselves talk more than they enjoy hearing others talk. But if you learn the keys to receiving messages and make a strong effort to use them with your wrestlers, you'll be surprised by what you've been missing.

Pay Attention

First, you must pay attention; you must want to hear what others have to communicate to you. That's not always easy when you're busy coaching and have many things competing for your attention. But in one-on-one or team meetings with wrestlers, you must focus on what they are telling you, both verbally and nonverbally. You'll be amazed at the little signals you pick up. Not only will this focused attention help you catch every word your wrestlers say, but you'll also notice their moods and physical states. In addition, you'll get an idea of your wrestlers' feelings toward you and their teammates.

Listen Carefully

How you receive messages from others, perhaps more than anything else you do, demonstrates how much you care for the sender and what that person has to tell you. If you care little for your wrestlers or have little regard for what they have to say, it will show in how you listen to them. You need to check yourself. Do you find your mind wandering to what you are going to do after practice while one of your wrestlers is talking to you? Do you frequently have to ask your wrestlers, "What did you say?" If so, you need to work on the receiving mechanics of listening. But if you find that you're missing the messages your wrestlers send, perhaps the most critical question you should ask yourself is this: "Do I care enough to be a coach?"

Providing Feedback

So far we've discussed separately the sending and receiving of messages. But we all know that senders and receivers switch roles several times during an interaction. One person initiates communication by sending a message to another person, who receives the message. The receiver then becomes the sender by responding to the person who sent the initial message. These verbal and nonverbal responses are called *feedback*.

Your wrestlers will look to you for feedback all the time. They will want to know how you think they are performing, what you think of their ideas, and whether their efforts please you. You can respond in many ways, and how you respond will strongly affect your wrestlers. They will react most favorably to positive feedback.

Praising wrestlers when they have performed or behaved well is an effective way to get them to repeat (or try to repeat) that behavior. And positive feedback for effort is an especially effective way to motivate youngsters to work on difficult skills. So rather than shouting at and providing negative feedback to wrestlers who have made mistakes, try to offer positive feedback and let them know what they did correctly and how they can improve. Sometimes just the way you word feedback can make it more positive than negative. For example, instead of saying, "Don't shoot from so far away," you might say, "Get closer before you attack." Then your wrestlers will focus on what to do instead of what not to do.

Positive feedback can be verbal or nonverbal. Telling young wrestlers, especially in front of teammates, that they have performed well is a great way to boost their confidence. And a pat on the back or a handshake communicates that you recognize a wrestler's performance.

Communicating With Other Groups

In addition to sending and receiving messages and providing proper feedback to your wrestlers, coaching also involves interacting with members of the coaching staff, parents, fans, game officials, and opposing coaches. If you don't communicate effectively with these groups, your coaching career will be unpleasant and short lived. So try the following suggestions for communicating with these groups.

Coaching Staff

Before you hold your first practice, the coaching staff should meet and discuss the roles and responsibilities that each coach will undertake during the year. Depending on the number of assistant coaches, the staff responsibilities can be divided into different areas. For example, it may be helpful to assign coaches to specific wrestlers or groups of wrestlers according to size, skill level, or maturity. The head coach has the final responsibility for all phases of practice and competition, but as much as possible, the assistant coaches should be responsible for their specific areas.

Before practices start, the coaching staff must also discuss and agree on terminology, plans for practice, areas of concentration, progression of developmental techniques, competition-day organization, method of communicating during practice and competitions, and match conditions. The coaches on your staff must present a united front and speak with one voice, and they must all take a similar approach to coaching, interaction with the athletes and parents, and interaction with one another. Disagreements should be discussed away from the mat, and each coach should have a say as the staff comes to an agreement.

Coaching Tip
Your coaching staff must be organized before practices and competitions. Work with your staff to ensure that tasks are completed. Each staff member should be responsible for a specific task in an effort to use time more efficiently. This will enable you to focus on the actual practice or match.

Parents

A wrestler's parents need to be assured that their child is under the direction of a coach who is both knowledgeable about the sport and concerned about the youngster's well-being. You can put their worries to rest by holding a pre-season parent-orientation meeting in which you describe your background and your approach to coaching (see "Preseason Meeting Topics").

Preseason Meeting Topics

1. Outline the paperwork that is needed:
   - Copy of the athlete's birth certificate
   - Completed athlete's application and payment record
   - Report card from the previous year
   - Participation agreement form (discussed in chapter 4)
   - Informed consent form (see appendix A)

2. Go over the inherent risks of wrestling and other safety issues.

3. Inform parents of the date and time that uniforms and equipment will be handed out.

4. Review the season practice schedule, including the date, location, and time of each practice.

5. Go over the proper gear and attire that should be worn at each practice session.

6. Discuss nutrition, hydration, and rest for athletes.

7. Explain the goals for the team.

8. Cover methods of communication: e-mail list, emergency phone numbers, interactive Web site, and so on.

9. Discuss ways that parents can help with the team.

10. Discuss standards of conduct for coaches, athletes, and parents.

11. Provide time for questions and answers.

If parents contact you with a concern during the season, listen to them closely and try to offer positive responses. If you need to communicate with parents, catch them after a practice, give them a phone call, or send a note through e-mail or the U.S. mail. Messages sent to parents through children are often lost, misinterpreted, or forgotten.

Fans

The stands probably won't be overflowing at your matches, which means that you'll more easily hear the few fans who criticize your coaching. When you hear something negative about the job you're doing, don't respond. Keep calm, consider whether the message has any value, and if not, forget it. Acknowledging critical, unwarranted comments from a fan during a match will only encourage others to voice their opinions. So put away your "rabbit ears" and communicate to fans, through your actions, that you are a confident, competent coach.

You must also prepare your wrestlers for fans' criticism. Tell your wrestlers that it is you, not the spectators, they should listen to. If you notice that one of your wrestlers is rattled by a fan's comment, reassure the wrestler that your evaluation is more objective and favorable—and the one that counts.

Officials

How you communicate with officials will have a great influence on the way your wrestlers behave toward them. Therefore, you must set a good example. Greet officials with a handshake, an introduction, and perhaps casual conversation about the upcoming match. Indicate your respect for them before, during, and after the match. Don't shout, make nasty remarks, or use disrespectful body gestures. Your wrestlers will see you do it, and they'll get the idea that such behavior is appropriate. Plus, if the official hears or sees you, the communication between the two of you will break down.

Opposing Coaches

Make an effort to visit with the coaches of the other teams before a tournament. During a match, don't get into a personal feud with the opposing coach. Remember, it's the kids, not the coaches, who are competing. And by getting along well with the opposing coach, you'll show your wrestlers that competition involves cooperation.

3

Understanding Rules and Equipment

I n earlier times, even in the 20th century, American folkstyle wrestling matches were won only by pinning the opponent by holding the shoulders to the mat for at least two seconds. Because of this, matches were sometimes very long. As the sport became more humane and time limits were set, it became apparent that not every match could end in a pin. To decide a winner when there was no pin, a system of points to be awarded for various maneuvers was developed, which continued to evolve into the rules of the sport used today. In short, rules were developed to protect the competitors and to provide for orderly and timely competitions.

At the youth level, most local clubs recognize American folkstyle wrestling, so we have focused on this style throughout this chapter and throughout this book. The other two styles are freestyle and Greco-Roman, but these are generally used only when wrestlers participate in international clubs (see "Wrestling Styles" for more information). This introduction to the basic rules of folkstyle wrestling won't cover every rule of the sport, but instead will give you what you need in order to work with wrestlers who are 6 to 14 years old. This chapter covers the basics of the sport, including the different styles of wrestling, mat specifications, and wrestling equipment. It also describes match rules and procedures and wraps things up with officiating and some of the most common officiating signals.

Wrestling Styles

In the United States, three types of wrestling styles are recognized and practiced at the youth level: folkstyle, freestyle, and Greco-Roman. Each style has different rules, but all have virtually the same ultimate objective: to take the opponent from the feet to the back and hold the shoulders to the mat. In folkstyle wrestling, the shoulders must remain down for at least two seconds, which means *to win by fall.*

Most young people compete in folkstyle because it is the style used in high school and college competitions in the Unites States, and most youth clubs are formed in support of these programs so that they can feed wrestlers into high school and even collegiate teams. The heart of folkstyle wrestling is the local youth club. These clubs are where young people are typically first introduced and exposed to the sport, and they are where they learn many of the basics. Often, high school coaches guide these clubs, providing the volunteer coaches with the basic instruction that will produce the style they coach in their high school program. The other two styles seen at the youth level, freestyle and Greco-Roman, are practiced around the world and are governed by FILA (Fédération Internationale des Luttes Associées), the international governing body for wrestling. In our country, these international styles are governed by USA Wrestling, the representative body to the U.S. Olympic Committee. USA Wrestling also provides competitions in folkstyle for youth.

Although many countries around the world have their own unique type of folkstyle wrestling, American folkstyle is unique to the United States. In the United States, folkstyle wrestlers work to get the opponent to the mat (the takedown), work to hold the opponent down and turn him or her onto the back (the ride), and then work to pin the shoulders to the mat (the fall). For folkstyle, riding is a large part of the competition (see chapter 9 for more information on rides). International freestyle and Greco-Roman styles emphasize the fall, and the rules encourage more risk but reward it highly. For these styles, simply riding without working to get the fall is not desired. Of the two international styles, freestyle wrestling is most similar to folkstyle, although it places less emphasis on control and more on turning the opponent's back toward the mat. The Greco-Roman style prohibits grasping the opponent's legs or using the legs to trip or hold the opponent. Because the legs can't be used to attack or defend, the Greco-Roman style can produce spectacular lifts and throws, which are highly rewarded with points.

The transition from folkstyle to the international styles is not difficult for a fundamentally sound wrestler. Wrestlers who go on to compete internationally are noted for being particularly well-conditioned, well-disciplined athletes. And this conditioning and discipline result partially from the demands of folkstyle, in which a wrestler must learn how to dominate, control, and wear down an opponent. Conditioning is a strong part of the fundamental approach of U.S. coaches, while other top nations emphasize skill and explosion rather than the aggressive style of the United States.

Mat

Youth folkstyle wrestling typically takes place on the same size and type of mat used for high school wrestling. The mat is made of vinyl-covered, shock-absorbent foam and is no more than 4 inches thick. The wrestling area of the mat is a circle with a diameter of at least 28 feet. It is outlined by a 2-inch-wide line. At the center of the wrestling area is another circle outlined with a 2-inch-wide line; it has a diameter of 10 feet. Inside the 10-foot circle are two 1-foot starting lines, one green and one red. They are connected by lines 3 feet long, 12 inches from the inside circle's lines. A 5-foot-wide protection zone surrounds the wrestling area. See figure 3.1.

Ideally, youth wrestling takes place on a regulation mat as described. However, at the youth level, it is common, especially in tournaments, to see full-sized mats divided into halves or quarters. A large tournament with several hundred competitors would be severely limited if it were held on full mats because most school gymnasiums can hold only three or four. If divided mats are used, the hosts should mark a 10-foot circle in the middle of each half or quarter, and direct the officials to work to ensure that most wrestling

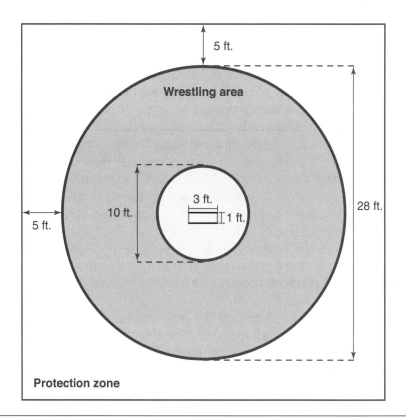

Figure 3.1   Youth wrestling mat.

takes place inside the circle. A 10-foot circle allows a generous protection zone to help ensure the safety of the competitors. The youngest age groups and lightest weight classes should be directed to the smallest mats, and officials and coaches must be prepared to protect the contestants from colliding with wrestlers on adjacent mats.

Wrestling Equipment

Standard equipment for youth wrestling includes shoes, uniform, headgear, and other appropriate apparel. But how do you know when this equipment meets proper specifications and is in good repair? You must examine the condition of each item you distribute to athletes. You must also make sure that the equipment they furnish themselves meets acceptability standards. Make sure that each wrestler on your team is outfitted properly and demonstrate to wrestlers how to properly wear their equipment. Following is additional information about the equipment used in wrestling:

- *Shoes.* Soft shoes with flat soles are required. The shoes may not have metal eyelets, and the rigid tips of shoelaces must be cut off. Many sportswear companies make wrestling-specific shoes. Commonly at the youth level, coaches allow kids to practice in regular athletic shoes if they are clean so that the youths can decide if they want to pursue wrestling. This keeps parents from having to purchase expensive gear before the kids know whether they will enjoy wrestling. High school, college, and international wrestling rules require laces to be taped over or covered so that matches are not stopped because laces become untied. Some youth competitions may require this also. If so, wrap athletic tape around the ankles of the shoes to cover the lace knots. This wrap does not need to be very tight—do not put the athlete's feet to sleep!

- *Uniform.* The one-piece uniform is called a *singlet,* under which athletes must wear underbriefs. Male wrestlers can wear an athletic supporter and female wrestlers, a sports bra. For practice, wrestlers usually wear shorts and a T-shirt with acceptable wrestling shoes. Singlets are worn for competitions. Ideally, shorts have no pockets; if they do, it is best if they are sewn shut because finger and thumb injuries can occur if wrestlers get their hands tangled in a practice partner's pocket while attacking.

- *Kneepads.* Kneepads are commonly worn in practices and matches. There are specific guidelines for kneepads and knee braces, so check with your club regarding these. Note that kneepads are not required for wrestlers, and parents should not feel the need to purchase them unless there is a specific medical reason for the wrestler to wear them.

- *Headgear.* Protective headgear is required and is encouraged for young athletes in wrestling competition. Headgear is not meant to protect against head injuries such as concussions. The purpose of headgear, also called ear guards, is to prevent wrestlers from damaging their ears. Ear injuries can lead to what is known as *cauliflower ear.* Cauliflower ear develops when the skin separates from the cartilage because of a blow or friction. The damage can lead to the formation of a hematoma, and left unattended, new cartilage may form. This can result in scarring that will sometimes look like the surface of a head of cauliflower. Young wrestlers are not prone to cauliflower ear, but they should be encouraged, and in most cases required, to practice and compete with headgear on. Most cauliflower ear is caused by heavy repetition and very physical wrestling found in higher levels of competition such as high school and college wrestling. If pain, redness, and swelling appear, send the wrestler to an experienced sports physician as soon as possible.

- *Special equipment.* Wrestlers may have an injury or situation that requires a special taping procedure, braces, protective goggles, elbow sleeves, and so on. Referees and coaches are required to examine all special equipment before each competition to ensure that it meets the requirements of the school or club. Please check your school or club rules to verify the legality and requirements of all special equipment.

Weight Classes

Local youth clubs may use several methods for grouping wrestlers for competition. Grouping wrestlers into weight classes is the most common method and was established in an attempt to create an equal opportunity for wrestlers to compete at their best level. Pairing weight classes with age groups helps keep wrestlers of similar maturity levels grouped together, and maturity may be as important a consideration as weight. You will encounter other methods as well.

Tournament organizers may sometimes group wrestlers less formally in an attempt to even out the number of wrestlers per competitive group. For example, if 24 wrestlers weighing 100 to 105 pounds, five wrestlers weighing 98 to 99 pounds, and 3 weighing 106 pounds weigh in, the pairing officials may split these 32 wrestlers into three groups instead of having such unbalanced numbers. This helps everyone get in a similar number of matches and keeps the tournament from dragging on at the end while one or two weight classes have many more matches than the others. In any case, the pairing officials will work to avoid mismatches because of excessive weight difference. Be vigilant and ask for change if there is too much disparity among athletes. The main concern of all officials and coaches should be the safety of the wrestlers and an enjoyable competition.

USA Wrestling has established youth age groups and assigned match time limits and weight classes for each group. Some state associations have expanded these to provide a framework for younger children. See table 3.1 for a list of the age groups and weights for youth wrestling as recommended by USA Wrestling.

Table 3.1   Match Durations and Weight Divisions for Youth Wrestling

Age group	Duration of match	Weight (lbs.)
Pee Wee (ages 6 and 7)	3 two-min. periods with a 30-sec. rest between periods	30, 35, 40, 45, 50, 55, 60, 65, 65+ (10 lbs. max. difference)
Bantam (ages 8 and 9)	3 two-min. periods with a 30-sec. rest between periods	40, 45, 50, 55, 60, 65, 70, 75, 75+ (15 lbs. max. difference)
Midget (ages 10 and 11)	3 two-min. periods with a 30-sec. rest between periods	50, 55, 60, 65, 70, 75, 80, 87, 95, 103, 112, 120, 120+ (20 lbs. max. difference)
Novice (ages 12 and 13)	3 two-min. periods with a 30-sec. rest between periods	60, 65, 70, 75, 80, 85, 90, 95, 100, 105, 112, 120, 130, 140, 140+ (25 lbs. max. difference)
Schoolboy/Schoolgirl (ages 14 and 15)	3 two-min. periods with a 30-sec. rest between periods	70, 75, 80, 85, 90, 95, 100, 105, 110, 115, 120, 125, 130, 145,165, 185, 205, 225, 250

Competition

Wrestling matches are opportunities for wrestlers to translate the skills they have learned in practice into a competition with other wrestlers. Youth wrestling has two principal forms of competition: tournaments and dual meets.

In tournaments, wrestlers from many clubs or teams compete in each weight class. Often there is more than one wrestler from the same club. Team scores are not usually kept in tournaments at the youth level, but there are awards for the wrestlers who win or place in the competition. USA Wrestling tournaments do not include team scoring except at the national championship level for older age groups. As competition moves to high school teams, tournament scoring becomes important.

Dual meets are competitions between two teams. Each team enters one wrestler per weight class, and he or she wrestles an opponent in that weight class from the other team. Team scoring is the idea behind dual meets, and the winning wrestler is awarded three to six points depending on the nature of the win. Individual points are totaled, and the team with the most points wins the dual competition.

Entering Competition

Although weight classes are different for different ages, the system for entering athletes into competitions is the same for all levels. In a dual meet, each team may enter one wrestler in each weight class. The same is true for invitational tournaments, where teams are invited and each enters one wrestler per weight class. However, in open tournaments, a school or club may enter as many wrestlers as it wishes, and wrestlers can sometimes enter as individuals, without club or team membership.

Clubs that host tournaments can make fliers available at other competitions, send fliers to the coaches of other clubs, and advertise in wrestling publications or on Web sites. Ads should specify location, rules to be observed, age groups competing, time and place of weigh-ins, and time and place of the competition. Generally, only statewide championships and USA Wrestling regional and national competitions require preregistration. Events sanctioned by USA Wrestling require that competitors hold an athlete membership card, and this must be presented when making an entry. This may be true of other governing bodies as well. Athletes register upon arriving at the site, and then go to the weigh-in room.

Weigh-Ins

A weigh-in is held before a competition to ensure that each athlete's body weight is within the limits of his or her weight class. This usually occurs at least an hour before the event's scheduled start time to allow tournament administrators time to organize the wrestlers into their weight classes and set up brackets. In some cases, weigh-ins are highly structured with all the wrestlers from a specific weight class standing in line to be weighed.

Medical personnel should check each athlete thoroughly for skin infections before he or she is allowed to weigh in. When cleared, the athlete reports for the weigh-in. USA Wrestling requires, as do some other organizations, that athletes weigh in wearing uniforms or shorts because officials may be women, and girls and women may enter some competitions. When the wrestler comes to the scale, the official confirms that the medical clearance is complete and then directs the wrestler to step on the scale. Digital scales are used most often now. When using a digital scale, the readout should not be visible to the athlete. This is done to keep the athlete from moving around on the scale in an attempt to affect the result. If a balance scale is used, the official should direct the athlete to stand in the middle of the platform and stand still. Most associations and leagues give an athlete just one chance on the scale. If athletes are over the allowed weight, they are not allowed to compete. It is the responsibility of the athlete and the coach to be sure that the stated weight is correct before presenting for weigh-in.

Match Structure

A match is made up of three timed periods. The time can vary depending on local rules. For example, USA Wrestling specifies three 2-minute periods with 30 seconds of rest between each period for all age categories (see table 3.1); however, some tournament organizers use 1-minute periods for the younger age groups. Before the start of a competition, check the rules to make sure you know what the time periods are for each age group.

The first period starts with both wrestlers standing. At the end of the first period, the official determines which wrestler gets to choose how to start the second period. If it is a dual meet, this protocol is decided before the first match, and the teams alternate who gets the choice. In a tournament, the athletes wear colored ankle bands to help the official and scorers identify athletes. The official flips a colored disc, and the wrestler with the winning color gets the choice.

The wrestler with the choice at the start of the second period has four options. Athletes can choose to defer the choice to their opponent so they can make the choice they want in the third period. They can choose to start in the neutral position, both wrestlers standing. They can choose to start down so that they can escape or get a reversal while they are still fresh. Finally, they can choose to start in the top position so they can work to get the fall, again, while fresh.

A match is over if one wrestler achieves a pin, or fall (see chapter 9 for more information on pins). Matches are also stopped if one wrestler gets ahead of the other by 15 or more points, a technical fall. Disqualification for misconduct, stalling, or other severe violations of the rules also stop a match. Although wrestling is one of the martial arts, or combat sports, any hold or maneuver applied with the intent to injure the opponent is prohibited.

Starting a Match

All youth wrestling matches begin with the two wrestlers on their feet, facing each other in a neutral position, with no advantage to either one. The duration of a match is specified according to the wrestling style and the age group involved.

Substitutions are not allowed during a match; however, for a dual meet, it is possible for two athletes to weigh in at the same weight so that you can choose which athlete to use when it is that weight group's turn to compete. Wrestling does not have a time-out in the way we understand them in basketball or football. There are no stops to be used strategically, to compose the team, or simply to catch a rest. It is possible for an athlete to ask for a time-out for injury. Injury time-outs have time limits, and once the time is reached, the athlete must compete or withdraw. The time limit is most often one and a half minutes. Different organizations allow a different number of injury time-outs. Coaches and wrestlers must know the rule for the specific competition before it begins. In college wrestling, for instance, only one time-out is allowed, and if the athlete asks for a second, the match is terminated.

The official will stop a match when blood is present so that the bleeding can be stopped and the wrestlers and the mat cleaned and disinfected. There is no time limit for blood issues, and the match will continue until it becomes clear that the bleeding is interfering with the match too much. The official can choose to stop the match at that point, and the wrestler who is not able to continue will take a loss.

Scoring

Depending on the starting position for each period, the wrestlers try to score takedowns, escapes, reversals, and near falls to control their opponents on the mat, to turn them over, and then to pin their shoulders for a fall. The successful execution of these maneuvers is rewarded with match points. To understand how the various maneuvers are scored, see table 3.2.

In folkstyle team competitions, wrestlers earn team points that contribute to the team's score. For team scoring, a win by a decision (victory by 1 to 7 points more than the opponent) is worth 3 points; a major decision (victory by 8 to 14 points), 4; a technical fall (victory by at least 15 points), 5; and a fall, 6. The loser receives no points. Winning by injury default, forfeit, or disqualification counts the same as a fall.

Officiating

Wrestling officials enforce the rules. Their authority over a match begins at least 30 minutes before the start of the match and finishes at least 30 minutes

Table 3.2   Match Scoring

Maneuver	Description	Points
Takedown	Taking the opponent, under control, from the neutral position to the mat	2
Escape	Escaping from the control of the top wrestler	1
Reversal	Reversing the control position	2
Near fall	Holding the opponent's shoulders in the near fall position (one shoulder on the mat and the other within 45 degrees of the mat)	2 points for 2 sec. or 3 points for 5 sec.
Fall	Holding both of the opponent's shoulders to the mat for two seconds	Winner of the match; or if the time limit for the match ends and neither wrestler has scored a fall, the winner is determined by the number of points earned

after it has ended. For most youth wrestling there is usually one mat official. In high school and college championship competition and for important college dual meets, there may also be an assistant official. Officials for youth competition may have a wide range of training and expertise. Because of this, pay close attention to the conduct of the match. You can learn a lot by watching a good, experienced official. You can also help an inexperienced official from time to time, but always do so respectfully.

Many youth competitions and most scholastic competitions will have three officials per mat—the referee, the timekeeper, and the scorekeeper. Some competitions, however, may be different. For example, as the tournaments get more serious or move into regional and state competition, the full complement of officials may include the timekeeper, the scorekeeper, the referee, the mat judge, and the mat chair. The referee, mat judge, and chair act together, and two of the three must agree for calls to stand.

Officials have many responsibilities during a match, including effectively communicating the calls to the scorers so the coaches, athletes, and spectators can understand the action. See figure 3.2 for common officiating signals.

If you have a concern about the officiating, always address the officials respectfully. They, like you, are most often volunteering their time and talent for the good of the wrestlers and the sport. Go to the scorer's table, and the official will come speak to you when there is a stop in the action. Do so immediately if at any time you feel that the officiating jeopardizes the safety of the athletes.

Figure 3.2 Officiating signals for *(a)* stop the match, *(b)* time-out, *(c)* start the injury clock, *(d)* stop the injury clock, *(e)* neutral position, *(f)* no control, *(g)* out of bounds, *(h)* wrestler in control (use either hand).

(continued)

Figure 3.2 *(continued) (i)* defer choice, *(j)* potentially dangerous move (use either hand), *(k)* stalemate, *(l)* caution for false start or incorrect starting position, *(m)* stalling (use either hand), *(n)* interlocking hands or grasping clothing, *(o)* reversal, *(p)* technical violation, *(q)* illegal hold or unnecessary roughness.

Figure 3.2 *(continued) (r)* near fall, *(s)* awarding points, *(t)* unsporting conduct, and *(u)* flagrant misconduct.

4

Providing for Wrestlers' Safety

As they review single-leg setups and finishes, Jason begins to work through takedowns with Carlos, giving Jason a good look at resistance. Jason brings Carlos to the mat, and at first everything seems to be normal. However, Carlos gets up slowly and obviously has pain in his shoulder. You ask Carlos to come over, and you quickly see he has an injury, maybe a collarbone fracture. What do you do?

No coach wants to see athletes get hurt. But injury remains a reality of sport participation; consequently, you must be prepared to provide first aid when injuries occur and to protect yourself against unjustified lawsuits. Fortunately, coaches can institute many preventive measures to reduce the risk. In this chapter we describe steps you can take to prevent injuries, first aid and emergency responses for when injuries occur, and your legal responsibilities as a coach.

Game Plan for Safety

You can't prevent every injury from happening, but you can take preventive measures that will give your athletes the best possible chance for injury-free participation. In creating the safest possible environment for your athletes, we'll explore what you can do in these areas:

- Preseason physical examination
- Physical conditioning
- Equipment and facilities inspection
- Athlete matchups and inherent risks
- Proper supervision and record keeping
- Environmental conditions

Preseason Physical Examination

We recommend that your athletes have a physical examination before participating in wrestling. The exam should address the most likely areas of medical concern and identify youngsters at high risk. We also suggest that you have athletes' parents or guardians sign a participation agreement (this will be discussed in more detail later in this chapter) and an informed consent form to allow their children to be treated in case of an emergency. For a sample form, please see "Informed Consent Form" in appendix A on page 177.

Physical Conditioning

Athletes need to be in or get in shape to perform at the level expected of them. They must have adequate cardiorespiratory fitness and muscular fitness.

Cardiorespiratory Fitness

Cardiorespiratory fitness involves the body's ability to use oxygen and fuels efficiently to power muscle contractions. A strong, well-conditioned cardiorespiratory system, which is made up of the heart, blood vessels, and lungs, enables your wrestlers' bodies to receive more oxygen and a higher volume of blood with every pump of the heart. It also allows wrestlers to sustain a high level of exertion longer and enhances both the youngster's health and wrestling performance.

As athletes get in better shape, their bodies are able to more efficiently deliver oxygen to fuel muscles and carry off carbon dioxide and other wastes. Wrestling requires lots of movement and short bursts of energy throughout a match. Youngsters who aren't as fit as their peers often overextend while trying to keep up, which can result in lightheadedness, nausea, fatigue, and potential injury. An excellent way to strengthen the cardiorespiratory system is to put it under controlled stress through a progressive increase in the intensity of aerobic exercise, which promotes the intake of oxygen. Cardiorespiratory benefits from aerobic activities, such as running, cycling, or circuit weight training, are produced when the athlete's heart rate remains at about 70 percent of its maximum for at least 25 minutes at least three times a week. To calculate this optimum heart rate, subtract the athlete's age in years from 220, then multiply by 70 percent. For example, to benefit aerobically from a workout, a 12-year-old should sustain a heart rate of 145 beats per minute for at least 25 minutes.

> **Coaching Tip**
> Each wrestler has unique hydration needs, so have water available at all times during practice sessions so wrestlers can grab a drink when they need it. In addition to being good for wrestlers, it also reduces the need for long water breaks during practices. However, younger wrestlers may not be aware that they need a break for water and a short rest; therefore, you should work breaks into your practice schedules.

Try to remember that the athletes' goals are to participate, learn, and have fun. Therefore, you must keep the wrestlers active, attentive, and involved with every phase of practice. If you do, they will attain higher levels of cardiorespiratory fitness as the season progresses simply by taking part in practice. However, watch closely for signs of low cardiorespiratory fitness; don't let your athletes overdo it as they build their fitness. You might privately counsel youngsters who appear overly winded, suggesting that they train under proper supervision outside of practice to increase their fitness.

Muscular Fitness

Muscular fitness encompasses flexibility, strength, speed, and balance. This type of fitness is affected by physical maturity, as well as strength training and other types of training. Your wrestlers will likely exhibit a relatively wide range of muscular fitness. Those who have greater muscular fitness will be able to wrestle with greater success. They will also sustain fewer muscular injuries, and any injuries that do occur will tend to be minor. And in case of injury, recovery is faster in those with higher levels of muscular fitness.

Flexibility   Although young bodies are generally very limber, they too can become tight through inactivity. Wrestling requires adequate range of motion at all body joints, and muscles that are tight and restrict movement not only limit performance but are also an injury waiting to happen.

From the very first practice session to the very last match, emphasize the importance of proper warm-up and cool-down to your wrestlers. When warming up, athletes should stimulate and lengthen each muscle group by stretching to the point of slight discomfort, then holding in that position for several counts. Stretch each muscle group at least three times, with a period of relaxation between stretches. If a wrestler's particular muscle group fails to loosen up after initial stretching, he or she should use it in a brief period of light activity, then attempt to stretch it again. When cooling down, wrestlers should take at least five minutes to stretch the muscles used during practice or competition so that they will be less tight before the next workout and so they will experience less muscle soreness.

Strength   The development of muscular strength through resistance training is an important part of total-body conditioning. The best conditioning tool for your wrestlers, along with running, is vigorous physical activity within a well-structured wrestling environment. Practicing skills, especially lifting (which is discussed in more detail in chapter 7), and participating in competition should provide much of the resistance work that wrestlers need.

However, you may find that some wrestlers benefit from following a training program designed to strengthen specific muscle groups. Any such program should be prepared by a qualified athletic trainer and tailored for the age group involved.

Speed and Balance   Some coaches believe that fitness and performance components are gifts of nature—athletes either have them or they don't. Included in the list of skills of a "natural athlete" are the components of speed and balance. However, don't give up quickly if your roster includes several slow-moving, stumbling wrestlers. Many informed coaches and countless athletes can attest to the fact that speed and balance can be improved through proper training. Routinely engage your wrestlers in activities during practice that focus on agility or require them to move in short bursts.

Equipment and Facilities Inspection

Another way to prevent injuries is to check the quality and fit of uniforms, practice attire, and protective equipment that your wrestlers use. Remember also to regularly examine the facilities in which your athletes practice and compete. Remove hazards, report conditions you cannot remedy, and request maintenance as necessary. If unsafe conditions exist, either make adaptations to prevent risk to your wrestlers' safety or stop the practice or match until safe conditions have been restored. Refer to appendix A for the "Facilities and Equipment Checklist" on page 176 to guide you in verifying that facilities are safe.

Choosing a Proper Weight Class

Wrestling is a sport for athletes of all shapes and sizes, which is one of the sport's greatest assets. However, the very weight-class system that allows both big and little athletes to achieve success also lends itself to abuse by wrestlers, coaches, and parents, specifically in the form of weight cutting and manipulation of body fluids. In youth wrestling especially, this behavior is harmful to the health of the wrestler and the reputation of the sport.

Wrestlers who are 12 years old and younger, well conditioned, and active should not cut weight. They are better served by working on technique and conditioning. However, wrestlers who are obviously carrying extra weight are encouraged to become leaner through diet and exercise. Their weight-loss program should be supervised and focus on leading a healthy lifestyle and becoming fit rather than focusing on reaching a lower weight class. Partner any weight-loss program with exercise that works on all major muscle groups. Without exercise, it is likely that youngsters will lose fat and muscle in roughly equal proportions; therefore, the athlete might lose weight, but the percentage of weight that is made up of lean tissue will not improve.

Youth wrestlers who are at least 13 years old could consider a small weight adjustment if it is properly supervised. State high school leagues have weight-reduction policies that you can use as a guide. Most are based on computing the lean mass of the wrestler, comparing to the preseason natural weight, and applying a time factor to regulate the rate and amount of reduction.

Before the wrestling season, each wrestler should have a preseason medical examination, and during this examination, a physician should assess the wrestlers' body fat percentage. Then before selecting an appropriate weight class for a wrestler, you should work with the parents and the family physician to determine the wrestler's optimal competitive weight. This optimal weight is neither the wrestler's lowest possible weight nor the weight at which he or she can best make the lineup. It should be the wrestler's healthiest weight—the one at which he or she can perform most effectively without slowing normal growth. If a physician determines that a weight-control program is necessary, it should start a couple of months before the official start of the wrestling season. For more information about weight classes and formal guidelines, please refer to page 24.

Athlete Matchups and Inherent Risks

Group teams in two-year age increments if possible. You'll encounter fewer mismatches in physical maturation with narrow age ranges. Even so, two 12-year-old boys might differ by 90 pounds in weight, a foot in height, and three or four years in emotional and intellectual maturity. Such variation presents dangers for the less mature. Closely supervise practices and matches so that the more mature kids do not put the less mature kids at undue risk.

Although proper matching of age groups helps protect you from certain liability concerns, you must also warn wrestlers of the inherent risks involved in wrestling; failure to warn is one of the most successful arguments in lawsuits against coaches. Thoroughly explain the inherent risks of wrestling and make sure each wrestler knows, understands, and appreciates the risks.

The preseason orientation meeting for parents is a good opportunity to explain the risks of the sport to both parents and wrestlers. It is also a good occasion on which to have both the wrestlers and their parents sign a participation agreement form or waiver releasing you from liability should an injury occur. Work with your school or club when creating these forms or waivers, and legal counsel should review them before presentation. These documents do not relieve you of responsibility for your wrestlers' well-being, but lawyers recommend them and they may help you in the event of a lawsuit.

Proper Supervision and Record Keeping

To ensure wrestlers' safety, you must provide both general supervision and specific supervision. General supervision means you are in the area where activity takes place so that you can see and hear what is happening. You should be

- in position to supervise the wrestlers even before the formal practice begins,
- immediately accessible to the activity and able to oversee the entire activity,
- alert to conditions that may be dangerous to wrestlers and ready to take action to protect wrestlers,
- able to react immediately and appropriately to emergencies, and
- present until the last wrestler has been picked up after the practice or match.

Specific supervision refers to the direct supervision of an activity at practice. For example, you should provide specific supervision when you teach new skills and continue it until your wrestlers understand the requirements of the activity, the risks involved, and their own ability to perform in light of these risks. This principle suggests that younger and less experienced wrestlers will require more specific supervision. And as a general rule, the more dangerous the activity, the more specific the supervision required. You must also provide specific supervision when you notice wrestlers breaking rules or see a change in their condition.

As part of your supervisory duties, you are expected to foresee potentially dangerous situations and help prevent them. This responsibility requires that you know wrestling well, especially the rules that are intended to provide for safety. For example, serious injury and possibly death can occur if a wrestler improperly performs a lifting technique on an opponent and does not return the opponent to the mat safely. Specific supervision applied consistently will make the environment safer for your wrestlers and will help protect you from liability if a mishap occurs.

For further protection, keep records of your season plans, practice plans, and wrestlers' injuries. Season and practice plans come in handy when you need evidence that you have taught wrestlers certain skills, and accurate, detailed injury report forms offer protection against unfounded lawsuits. Ask for these forms from your sponsoring organization (see "Injury Report Form" in appendix A on page 178), and hold onto these records for several years so that a so-called old wrestling injury of a former wrestler doesn't come back to haunt you.

Coaching Tip

Although younger age groups need quite a bit of supervision during practices and matches, they typically do not generate the force or velocity necessary to cause impact injuries that teenage wrestlers do. They bump into one another, which may cause a few sniffles, but it is less likely to cause a serious injury. You must attentively supervise all activity of all age groups at all training sessions and matches.

Environmental Conditions

Even though wrestling is typically an indoor sport, environmental conditions can affect your wrestlers, and these effects can carry over into the wrestling room or gym. Most health problems caused by environmental factors are related to excessive heat or cold, although you should also consider other environmental factors such as severe weather and air pollution. A little thought about the potential problems and a little effort to ensure adequate protection for your athletes will prevent most serious emergencies related to environmental conditions.

Heat

For wrestling, heat can come into play. The NCAA has mandated that college and university wrestling rooms be at or below 75 degrees Fahrenheit, and they do not allow the use of steam rooms, saunas, or vapor-impermeable clothing, such as rubber suits or "plastics," that trap extreme amounts of heat and prevent the body from cooling through perspiration. USA Wrestling has also disallowed the use of this type of clothing. Very warm rooms or excessive clothing or both stimulate perspiration, but after some time, they also reduce a young wrestler's ability to practice well. Anything that builds heat or exhaustion to the point that young athletes cannot execute proper technique should be discouraged.

On hot, humid days, the body has difficulty cooling itself. Because the air is already saturated with water vapor (humidity), sweat doesn't evaporate as easily. Therefore, body sweat is a less effective cooling agent, and the body retains extra heat. Hot, humid environments put wrestlers at risk of heat exhaustion and heatstroke (see more on these in "Serious Injuries" on pages 46 to 48). And if *you* think it's hot or humid, it's worse for the kids, not only because they're more active, but also because kids under the age of 12 have more difficulty regulating their body temperature than adults do.

Coaching Tip

Encourage wrestlers to drink plenty of water before, during, and after practice. Water makes up 45 to 65 percent of a youngster's body weight, and even a small amount of water loss can cause severe consequences in the body's systems. It doesn't have to be hot and humid for wrestlers to become dehydrated, nor is thirst an accurate indicator. In fact, by the time wrestlers are aware of their thirst, they are long overdue for a drink.

To provide for wrestlers' safety in hot or humid conditions, take the following preventive measures. Table 4.1 lists some warm-weather precautions for different temperatures.

- Monitor weather conditions and adjust training sessions accordingly.
- Acclimatize wrestlers to exercising in high heat and humidity. Athletes can adjust to high heat and humidity in 7 to 10 days. During this period, hold practices at low to moderate activity levels and give the wrestlers fluid breaks every 20 minutes.
- Switch to light clothing. Athletes should wear shorts and white T-shirts, or check with your governing body for other clothing suggestions.
- Identify and monitor wrestlers who are prone to heat illness. This would include participants who are overweight, heavily muscled, or out of shape and wrestlers who work excessively hard or have suffered previous heat illness. Closely monitor these wrestlers and give them fluid breaks every 15 to 20 minutes.
- Make sure wrestlers replace fluids lost through sweat. Encourage them to drink 17 to 20 ounces of fluid two to three hours before each practice or match, to drink 7 to 10 ounces every 20 minutes during practice and after practice, and to drink 16 to 24 ounces of fluid for every pound lost. Fluids such as water and sports drinks are preferable during practices and matches (suggested intakes are based on NATA [National Athletic Trainers' Association] recommendations).
- Encourage wrestlers to replenish electrolytes, such as sodium (salt) and potassium, that are lost through sweat. The best way to replace these nutrients—as well as others such as carbohydrate (which provides energy) and protein (which builds muscle)—is by eating a balanced diet. Experts say that additional salt intake may be helpful during the most intense training periods in the heat.

Table 4.1   Warm-Weather Precautions

Temperature (°F)	Humidity	Precautions
80-90	< 70%	Monitor athletes prone to heat illness
80-90	> 70%	5 min. rest after 30 min. of practice
90-100	< 70%	5 min. rest after 30 min. of practice
90-100	> 70%	Short practices in evenings or early morning

Cold

Although wrestling practices and competitions are held indoors, cold weather may be a factor as your wrestlers arrive for and leave practices and competitions. When a person is exposed to cold weather, body temperature starts to drop below normal. To counteract this reaction, the body shivers to create heat and reduces blood flow to the extremities to conserve heat in the core of the body. But no matter how effective its natural heating mechanism is, the body will better withstand cold temperatures if it is prepared to handle them. To reduce the risk of cold-related illnesses, keep wrestlers active to maintain body heat, and make sure they wear appropriate clothing. Also monitor the windchill factor because it can drastically affect the severity of wrestlers' responses to the weather. The windchill factor index is shown in figure 4.1.

Temperature (°F)

	0	5	10	15	20	25	30	35	40
	Flesh may freeze within one minute								
40	-55	-45	-35	-30	-20	-15	-5	0	10
35	-50	-40	-35	-30	-20	-10	-5	5	10
30	-50	-40	-30	-25	-20	-10	0	5	10
25	-45	-35	-30	-20	-15	-5	0	10	15
20	-35	-30	-25	-15	-10	0	5	10	20
15	-30	-25	-20	-10	-5	0	10	15	25
10	-20	-15	-10	0	5	10	15	20	30
5	-5	0	5	10	15	20	25	30	35

Wind speed (mph)

Windchill temperature (°F)

Figure 4.1   Windchill factor index.

Severe Weather

Again, although wrestling practices and competitions are held indoors, sudden severe weather as your wrestlers arrive for or leave practices or competitions could include a host of potential dangers, including lightning storms, tornadoes, hail, and heavy rains. When outdoors at any time, lightning is of special concern because it can come up quickly and can cause great harm or even kill. For each 5-second count from the flash of lightning to the bang of thunder, lightning is one mile away. A count of 10 seconds means lightning is two miles away; a count of 15 seconds indicates lightning is three miles away. In the case that you are outdoors at any time, a practice or competition should be stopped for the day if lightning is three miles away or closer (15 seconds or fewer from flash to bang). In addition to these suggestions, your school, league, or state association may also have additional rules that you will want to consider in severe weather.

Safe places in which to take cover when lightning strikes are fully enclosed metal vehicles with the windows up, enclosed buildings, and low ground (under cover of bushes, if possible). It's not safe to be near metal objects such as flagpoles, fences, light poles, and metal bleachers. Also avoid trees, water, and open fields.

Practices and competitions should be canceled when under a tornado watch or warning. If you are practicing or competing when a tornado is nearby, stay in the building. If for some reason you are outside, and you cannot get into a building, lie in a ditch or other low-lying area, or crouch near a strong building. Use your arms to protect your head and neck and instruct athletes to do the same.

The keys to handling severe weather are caution and prudence. If you are outside for conditioning exercises, come in if lightning is on the horizon or it is raining heavily. Many storms can strike both quickly and ferociously. Respect the weather and play it safe.

Air Pollution

If you're working on conditioning activities outside, poor air quality and smog can present real dangers to your wrestlers. Both short- and long-term lung damage are possible from participating in unsafe air. Although it's true that participating in clean air is not possible in many areas, restricting activity is recommended when the air quality ratings are lower than moderate or when there is a smog alert. Your local health department or air-quality control board can inform you of the air-quality ratings for your area and when restricting activities is recommended.

Responding to Injuries

No matter how good and thorough your prevention program is, injuries most likely will occur. When injury does strike, chances are you will be the one in charge. The severity and nature of the injury will determine how actively involved you'll be in treating it. But regardless of how seriously an athlete is hurt, it is your responsibility to know what steps to take. Therefore, you must be prepared to take appropriate action and provide basic emergency care when an injury occurs.

Being Prepared

Being prepared to provide basic emergency care involves many things, including being trained in cardiopulmonary resuscitation (CPR) and first aid, having a first aid kit on hand, and having an emergency plan.

CPR and First Aid Training

We recommend that all coaches receive CPR and first aid training from a nationally recognized organization such as the National Safety Council, the American Heart Association, the American Red Cross, or the American Sport

First Aid Kit

A well-stocked first aid kit should include the following:

- Antibacterial soap or wipes
- Arm sling
- Athletic tape—one and a half inches wide
- Bandage scissors
- Bandage strips—assorted sizes
- Blood spill kit
- Cell phone
- Contact lens case
- Cotton swabs
- Elastic wraps—three inches, four inches, and six inches
- Emergency blanket
- Examination gloves—latex-free
- Eye patch
- Foam rubber—one-eighth inch, one-fourth inch, and one-half inch
- Insect sting kit
- List of emergency phone numbers
- Mirror
- Moleskin
- Nail clippers
- Oral thermometer
- Penlight
- Petroleum jelly
- Plastic bags for crushed ice
- Prewrap (underwrap for tape)
- Rescue breathing or CPR face mask
- Safety glasses (for first aiders)
- Safety pins
- Saline solution for eyes
- Sterile gauze pads—three-inch and four-inch squares (preferably non-stick)
- Sterile gauze rolls
- Sunscreen—sun protection factor (SPF) 30 or greater
- Tape adherent and tape remover
- Tongue depressors
- Tooth saver kit
- Triangular bandages
- Tweezers

Adapted, by permission, from M. Flegel, 2004, *Sport first aid*, 3rd ed. (Champaign, IL: Human Kinetics), 20.

Education Program (ASEP). You should be certified based on a practical test and a written test of knowledge. CPR training should include pediatric and adult basic life support and obstructed-airway procedures.

Emergency Plan

An emergency plan is the final step in being prepared to take appropriate action for severe or serious injuries. The plan calls for three steps:

1. *Evaluate the injured athlete.*

   Use your CPR and first aid training to guide you. Be sure to keep these certifications up to date. Practice your skills frequently to keep them fresh and ready to use.

2. *Call the appropriate medical personnel.*

If possible, delegate the responsibility of seeking medical help to another calm and responsible adult who attends all practices and matches. Write out a list of emergency phone numbers and keep it with you at practices and matches. Include the following phone numbers:

- Rescue unit
- Hospital
- Physician
- Police
- Fire department

Take each athlete's emergency information to every practice and match (see "Emergency Information Card" in appendix A on page 179). This information includes the person to contact in case of an emergency, what types of medications the athlete is using, what types of drugs the athlete is allergic to, and so on.

Give an emergency response card (see "Emergency Response Card" in appendix A on page 180) to the contact person calling for emergency assistance. Having this information ready should help the contact person remain calm. You must also complete an injury report form (see appendix A on page 178) and keep it on file for any injury that occurs.

3. *Provide first aid.*

If medical personnel are not on hand at the time of the injury, provide first aid care to the extent of your qualifications. Again, although your CPR and first aid training will guide you, you must remember the following:

- Do not move the injured athlete if the injury is to the head, neck, or back; if a large joint (ankle, knee, elbow, shoulder) is dislocated; or if the pelvis, a rib, or an arm or leg is fractured.
- Calm the injured athlete and keep others away as much as possible.
- Evaluate whether the athlete's breathing has stopped or is irregular, and if necessary, clear the airway with your fingers.
- If the athlete is not breathing normally, or you are unsure, perform CPR.
- Remain with the athlete until medical personnel arrive.

Taking Appropriate Action

Proper CPR and first aid training, a well-stocked first aid kit, and an emergency plan help prepare you to take appropriate action when an injury occurs. In the previous section, we mentioned the importance of providing first aid to the extent of your qualifications. Don't "play doctor" with injuries; sort out

Emergency Steps

You must have a clear, well-rehearsed emergency action plan. You want to be sure you are prepared in case of an emergency because every second counts. Your emergency plan should follow this sequence:

1. Check the athlete's level of responsiveness.
2. Send a contact person to call the appropriate medical personnel and to call the athlete's parents if they are not present.
3. Send someone to wait for the rescue team and direct them to the injured athlete.
4. Assess the injury.
5. Administer first aid.
6. Assist emergency medical personnel in preparing the athlete for transportation to a medical facility.
7. Appoint someone to go with the athlete if the parents are not available. This person should be responsible, calm, and familiar with the athlete. Assistant coaches or parents are best for this job.
8. Complete an injury report form while the incident is fresh in your mind.

minor injuries that you can treat from those that need medical attention. Now let's look at taking the appropriate action for minor injuries and more serious injuries.

Minor Injuries

Although no injury seems minor to the person experiencing it, most injuries are neither life threatening nor severe enough to restrict participation. When these injuries occur, you can take an active role in their initial treatment.

Scrapes and Cuts   When one of your athletes has an open wound, the first thing you should do is put on a pair of disposable latex-free examination gloves or some other effective blood barrier. Then follow these four steps:

1. Stop the bleeding by applying direct pressure with a clean dressing to the wound and elevating it. The athlete may be able to apply this pressure while you put on your gloves. Do not remove the dressing if

Coaching Tip

You shouldn't let a fear of acquired immune deficiency syndrome (AIDS) and other communicable diseases stop you from helping an athlete. You are only at risk if you allow contaminated blood to come in contact with an open wound on your body, so the examination gloves that you wear will protect you from AIDS if one of your athletes carries this disease. Check with your sport director, your club, or the Centers for Disease Control and Prevention (CDC) for more information about protecting yourself and your participants from AIDS.

it becomes soaked with blood. Instead, place an additional dressing on top of the one already in place. If bleeding continues, elevate the injured area above the heart and maintain pressure.

2. Cleanse the wound thoroughly once the bleeding is controlled. A good rinsing with a forceful stream of water and perhaps light scrubbing with soap will help prevent infection.

3. Protect the wound with sterile gauze or a bandage strip. If the athlete continues to participate, apply protective padding over the injured area.

4. Remove and dispose of gloves carefully to prevent you or anyone else from coming into contact with blood.

For bloody noses not associated with serious facial injury, have the athlete sit and lean slightly forward. Then pinch the athlete's nostrils shut. If the bleeding continues after several minutes, or if the athlete has a history of nosebleeds, seek medical assistance.

Strains and Sprains   The physical demands of wrestling often result in injury to the muscles or tendons (strains) or to the ligaments (sprains). When your athletes suffer minor strains or sprains, immediately apply the PRICE method of injury care:

P	Protect the athlete and the injured body part from further danger or trauma.
R	Rest the injured area to avoid further damage and foster healing.
I	Ice the area to reduce swelling and pain.
C	Compress the area by securing an ice bag in place with an elastic wrap.
E	Elevate the injury above heart level to keep the blood from pooling in the area.

Bumps and Bruises   Inevitably, wrestlers make contact with each other and with the mat. If the force applied to a body part at impact is great enough, a bump or bruise will result. Many wrestlers continue participating with such sore spots, but if the bump or bruise is large and painful, take appropriate action. Again, use the PRICE method for injury care and monitor the injury. If swelling, discoloration, and pain have lessened, the athlete may resume participation with protective padding; if not, the athlete should be examined by a physician.

Serious Injuries

Head, neck, and back injuries; fractures; and injuries that cause an athlete to lose consciousness are among a class of injuries that you cannot and should not try to treat yourself. In these cases, you should follow the emergency plan outlined on pages 43 to 44. We do want to examine more closely, however, your role in preventing heat cramps, heat exhaustion, and heatstroke. Additionally, please refer to figure 4.2 for an illustrative example of the signs and symptoms associated with heat exhaustion and heatstroke.

Heat Cramps   Tough practices combined with heat stress and substantial fluid loss from sweating can provoke muscle cramps commonly known as *heat cramps*. Depending on your location, it may be hot early in the season, which can be problematic because athletes may be less conditioned and less adapted to heat, or later in the season, when athletes are better conditioned, but still not used to high temperatures. A cramp, a severe tightening of the muscle, can drop athletes and prevent continued wrestling. Dehydration, electrolyte loss, and fatigue are the contributing factors. The immediate treatment consists of having the athlete cool off and slowly stretch the contracted muscle. The athlete may return later that same day or the next day provided the cramp doesn't cause a muscle strain.

Heat Exhaustion   Heat exhaustion is a shocklike condition caused by dehydration and electrolyte depletion. Symptoms include headache, nausea, dizziness, chills, muscle cramps, fatigue, diarrhea, and extreme thirst. Profuse sweating is a key sign of heat exhaustion. Other signs include pale, cool, and clammy skin; rapid, weak pulse; loss of coordination; and dilated pupils.

An athlete suffering from heat exhaustion should rest in a cool area; drink cool fluids, particularly those containing electrolytes; and apply ice to the neck, back, or abdomen to help cool the body. If you believe an athlete has heat exhaustion, seek medical attention. Under no conditions should the athlete return to activity that day or before he or she regains all the weight lost through sweat. If the athlete has to see a physician, the athlete shouldn't return to the team until he or she has a written release from the physician.

Heatstroke   Heatstroke is a life-threatening condition in which the body stops sweating and body temperature rises dangerously high. It occurs when dehydration causes a malfunction in the body's temperature control center in the brain. Symptoms include the feeling of being extremely hot, headache, dizziness, nausea, confusion, irritability, and fatigue. Signs include hot, dry, and flushed or red skin (this is a key sign); heavy sweat or a lack of sweat; rapid pulse; rapid breathing; constricted pupils; vomiting; diarrhea; and possibly seizures, unconsciousness, or respiratory or cardiac arrest.

If you suspect that an athlete is suffering from heatstroke, send for emergency medical assistance immediately and cool the athlete as quickly as possible. Remove excess clothing and equipment from the athlete, and cool the wrestler's body with cool, wet towels; by pouring cool water over the body; or by placing

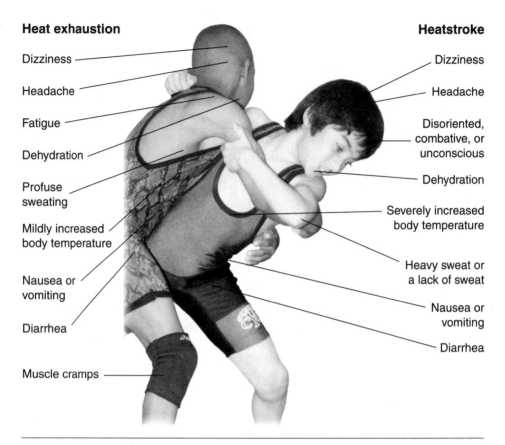

Heat exhaustion

Dizziness

Headache

Fatigue

Dehydration

Profuse sweating

Mildly increased body temperature

Nausea or vomiting

Diarrhea

Muscle cramps

Heatstroke

Dizziness

Headache

Disoriented, combative, or unconscious

Dehydration

Severely increased body temperature

Heavy sweat or a lack of sweat

Nausea or vomiting

Diarrhea

Figure 4.2   Signs and symptoms of heat exhaustion and heatstroke.

the athlete in a cold-water bath. Apply ice packs to the armpits, neck, back, abdomen, and between the legs. If the athlete is conscious, give him or her cool fluids to drink. If the athlete is unconscious, place the athlete on the side to allow fluids and vomit to drain from the mouth. An athlete who has suffered heatstroke may not return to the team until he or she has a written release from a physician.

Protecting Yourself

When one of your athletes is injured, naturally your first concern is the athlete's well-being. Your feelings for youngsters, after all, are what made you decide to coach. Unfortunately, you must also consider something else: Can you be held liable for the injury?

From a legal standpoint, a coach must fulfill nine duties. We've discussed all but planning the activity in this chapter (planning is discussed in chapters 5 and 11). The following is a summary of your legal duties:

1. Provide a safe environment.
2. Properly plan the activity.
3. Provide adequate and proper equipment.
4. Match athletes appropriately.
5. Warn of inherent risks in the sport.
6. Supervise the activity closely.
7. Evaluate athletes for injury or incapacitation.
8. Know emergency procedures, CPR, and first aid.
9. Keep adequate records.

In addition to fulfilling these nine legal duties, you should check your organization's insurance coverage and your own insurance coverage to make sure these policies will properly protect you from liability.

5

Making Practices Fun and Practical

I n the past we have placed too much emphasis on learning skills and not enough on learning how to wrestle skillfully—that is, how to use those skills in competition. The *games approach*, in contrast to the traditional approach, emphasizes learning what to do first, then how to do it. Moreover, the games approach lets kids discover what to do in competition not by your telling them, but by their experiencing it. It is a guided-discovery method of teaching that empowers your kids to solve the problems that arise in a match, which is a large part of the fun in learning.

On the surface, it seems to make sense to introduce wrestling by using the traditional approach of first teaching the basic skills of the sport and then the tactics of the sport, but it has been discovered that this approach has disadvantages. First, it teaches the skills of the sport outside of the context of a match. Kids may learn to shoot and sprawl, but then find it difficult to use these skills in a real match. This is because they do not yet understand the fundamental tactics of wrestling and do not appreciate how best to use their newfound skills. Second, learning skills by performing drills outside the context of the sport is downright boring. The single biggest turnoff in sports is overorganized instruction that deprives kids of their intrinsic desire to wrestle.

The games approach is taught using a four-step process:

1. Perform a modified activity.
2. Help the athletes understand the activity.
3. Teach the skills of the activity.
4. Practice the skills in another activity.

Step 1: Perform a Modified Activity

It's the first day of practice; some of the kids are eager to get started, while others are obviously apprehensive. Some have seen a real wrestling match, most don't know the rules, and few know the holds and maneuvers that are used in the sport. What do you do?

Using the traditional approach, you would start with a quick warm-up activity, then line up the wrestlers for a simple penetration-step drill and go from there. With the games approach, however, you begin by performing a modified activity that is developmentally appropriate for the wrestlers' level and focuses on learning a specific part of the sport of wrestling.

Modified wrestling emphasizes a limited number of situations. This is one way to guide your wrestlers' discovery of certain tactics in the sport. For instance, wrestlers participate in a sumo drill in which two participants try to move each other out of an eight-foot circle. This activity teaches the wrestlers about balance and control while attacking their opponent and forces them to think about what they have to do to set up an effective attack.

Activities Checklist

When developing activities for your youth wrestling program, ask yourself the following questions.

- Are the activities fun?
- Are the activities organized?
- Are the wrestlers involved in the activities?
- Do the activities require creativity and decision making?
- Are the spaces used appropriate?
- Is my feedback appropriate?
- Are there implications for competition?

Step 2: Help the Athletes Understand the Activity

As your wrestlers perform an activity, look for the right spot to freeze the action, step in, and ask questions about errors that you see. This helps them better understand the objective of the activity, what they must do to achieve the objective, and also what skills they must use to achieve the objective.

Asking the right questions is an important part of your teaching. You'll ask your wrestlers—usually literally—"What do you need to do to succeed in this situation?" Sometimes wrestlers simply need to have more time to perform the activity, or they may need you to modify the activity further so that they can discover what they should do. It may take more patience on your part, but it's a powerful way to learn. For example, assume your wrestlers are performing an activity in which the objective is to keep the opponent broken down flat on his or her belly, but they are having trouble maintaining a breakdown position. Interrupt the action and ask the following questions:

- What are you supposed to do in this activity?
- What do you have to do to keep the bottom wrestler facedown?
- How can you use your feet to help keep your opponent down?
- What parts of your body do you use to put weight on your opponent?

Coaching Tip

If your wrestlers have trouble understanding what to do, phrase questions into a choice between options. For example, if you ask them, "What is the best way to keep an opponent on his belly?" and your wrestlers answer "Lay on them," then rephrase your question so that it gives them a choice such as, "Is it better to use your arms or legs to create pressure on the defender?"

At first, asking the right questions might seem difficult because your wrestlers have little or no experience with the sport. And, if you've learned sport through the traditional approach, you'll be tempted to tell your wrestlers how to wrestle rather than taking the time to ask questions. In the games approach, however, resist this powerful temptation to tell your wrestlers what to do.

Instead, through modified activities and skillful questioning on your part, your wrestlers should come to the realization on their own that solid skills and tactical awareness are important for becoming a good wrestler. Leading your wrestlers to this discovery, rather than telling them what the critical skills are, is a crucial part of the games approach.

Step 3: Teach the Skills of the Activity

Only after your wrestlers are able to recognize the skills they need to be successful in the sport should you teach these skills through focused activities that simulate a specific match situation. This is when you will use a more traditional approach to teaching sport skills: the IDEA approach, which is described in chapter 6. This type of teaching breaks down the sport skills and should be implemented early in the season so wrestlers can begin attaining these skills, which makes the activities more fun.

Step 4: Practice the Skills in Another Activity

You want your wrestlers to experience success as they're learning skills, and the best way for them to experience success early is for you to create an advantage for them. Once the wrestlers have practiced the skill, as outlined in step 3, you can then put them in another situation—this time with an advantage for the top wrestler. For example, you may choose to start the bottom wrestler on his or her side. The top wrestler has a half nelson in place and is working for the turn and fall. In this case, the attacking—top—wrestler has a strong probability of success because his opponent is already at a disadvantage.

In another situation, one wrestler is deep in on a double-leg takedown, and his or her defender is standing nearly upright. You could start the attacker on his or her feet, locked around the opponent's legs; on one knee with the trail leg up, ready to cut the angle on his or her opponent; or with both knees on the mat, forcing the attacker to get up off the knees so that one wrestler has an advantage. This introduces wrestlers to situations similar to what they will experience in competition and lets them discover the challenges they will face in performing the skill. After they have experienced the situation, teach them the appropriate skill, let them practice it, and put them on the mat in another activity, creating an advantage that gives them a chance to experience success.

As wrestlers improve their skills, you may not need to provide an advantage. When this time comes, eliminate the advantage in practice, or you may even decide that they're ready to use the skill in regular competition. The key is to set up situations in which your wrestlers can experience success while still being challenged. This requires careful monitoring on your part, but having kids participate in modified activities as they learn skills is an effective way to help them learn and improve.

And that's the games approach. Your wrestlers will get to participate more in practice, and once they learn how the skills fit into their performance and enjoyment of the sport, they'll be more motivated to work on those skills, which will help them to be successful.

Coaching Tip
Make it a habit to end each practice with an activity that all of your athletes can have fun with and be successful at. This allows your athletes to leave practice in a positive frame of mind so that they will look forward to returning to the next practice.

6

Teaching and Shaping Skills

Coaching wrestling is about teaching kids the sport by teaching them skills, fitness, fair play, and values. It's also about coaching wrestlers before, during, and after matches. Teaching and coaching are closely related, but important differences exist. In this chapter we focus on the principles of teaching, especially teaching technical and tactical skills. But these principles apply to teaching fitness concepts and values as well. Armed with these principles, you will be able to design effective and efficient practices and will understand how to deal with misbehavior. Then you will be able to teach the skills necessary to be successful in wrestling, which are outlined in chapters 7 through 9.

Teaching Wrestling Skills

Many people believe that the only qualification needed to teach a skill is to have performed it. Although it's helpful to have performed the skill, teaching it successfully requires much more than that. Even if you haven't performed the skill before, you can still learn to teach successfully by using the acronym IDEA:

I   Introduce the skill.

D   Demonstrate the skill.

E   Explain the skill.

A   Attend to athletes practicing the skill.

Introduce the Skill

Athletes, especially those who are young and inexperienced, need to know what skill they are learning and why they are learning it. You should therefore use the following three steps every time you introduce a skill to your athletes:

1. Get your athletes' attention.
2. Name the skill.
3. Explain the importance of the skill.

Get Your Athletes' Attention

Because youngsters are easily distracted, you must make them sit up and take notice. Some coaches use interesting news items or stories, others use jokes, and still others simply project enthusiasm to get their athletes to listen. Whatever method you use, speak slightly above your normal volume and look your athletes in the eye when you speak.

Also, position athletes so that they can see and hear you. Arrange them in two or three evenly spaced rows, facing you (make sure they aren't looking at a distracting activity). Then ask whether all of them can see you before you begin to speak.

Name the Skill

Although the skill you will introduce may have several common names, decide as a staff before the start of the season which one you'll use and stick with it. Doing so prevents confusion and enhances communication among your athletes. When you introduce the new skill, call it by name several times so that the athletes automatically correlate the name with the skill in later discussions.

Coaching Tip

Writing out in detail each skill you will teach clarifies what you will say and how you will demonstrate each skill to your wrestlers.

Explain the Importance of the Skill

As Rainer Martens, the founder of ASEP, has said, "The most difficult aspect of coaching is this: Coaches must learn to let athletes learn. Sport skills should be taught so they have meaning to the child, not just meaning to the coach." Although the importance of a skill may be apparent to you, your athletes may be less able to see how the skill will help them become better wrestlers. Offer them a reason to learn the skill and describe how it relates to more advanced skills. Kids at least 10 years old should be able to understand straightforward explanations, and these explanations increase in importance as your wrestlers get older. However, when working with wrestlers 9 and younger, appeal to their imagination and use storytelling to introduce skills into matchlike activities.

Demonstrate the Skill

Demonstration is the most important part of teaching a sport skill to athletes who may never have done anything closely resembling it. They need to see how the skill is performed, not just to hear a description. If you are unable to perform the skill correctly, ask an assistant coach, one of your wrestlers, or someone more skilled to demonstrate it.

These tips will make your demonstrations more effective:

- Use correct form.
- Demonstrate the skill several times.
- Slow the action, if possible, during one or two performances so that athletes can see every movement involved in the skill.
- Perform the skill at different angles so that your athletes get a range of perspectives.
- Demonstrate the skill with both sides of the body, as applicable.

Coaching Tip

To keep the wrestlers' attention, demonstrations should take one minute or less. When working with 9- and 10-year-olds, try to keep demonstrations 30 seconds or shorter. When working with 6- to 8-year-olds, demonstrations should take no more than 15 seconds.

- Do not speak during the demonstration; save your words for before and after you demonstrate.

Explain the Skill

Athletes learn more effectively when they're given a brief explanation of the skill along with the demonstration. Use simple terms and, if possible, relate the skill to those previously learned. Ask your athletes whether they understand your description. A good technique is to ask the team to repeat your explanation. Ask questions like "What are you going to do first?" and "Then what?" Should athletes look confused or uncertain, repeat your explanation and demonstration. If possible, use different words so that your athletes can try to understand the skill from a different perspective. Remember, too, that whenever you bring athletes into a group to make a coaching point, you must be clear and concise.

Complex skills often are better understood when you explain them in more manageable parts. For instance, if you want to teach your athletes how to shoot a high-crotch takedown, you might take the following steps:

1. Show athletes a correct performance of the entire skill and explain its function.
2. Break down the skill and point out its component parts.
3. Have athletes perform each of the component skills you have already taught them, such as the setup, the level change, the proper hand position on the leg, and the finish or lift.
4. After athletes have demonstrated their ability to perform the separate parts of the skill in sequence, explain the entire skill again.
5. Have athletes practice the skill in matchlike conditions.

Young athletes have short attention spans, and a long demonstration or explanation of a skill may cause them to lose focus. Therefore, spend no more than a few minutes altogether on the introduction, demonstration, and explanation phases. Then involve the athletes in activities that call on them to perform the skill.

Attend to Athletes Practicing the Skill

If the skill you selected was within your athletes' capabilities and you have done an effective job of introducing, demonstrating, and explaining it, your athletes should be ready to attempt the skill. Some athletes may need to be physically guided through the movements during their first few attempts. Walking unsure athletes through the skill in this way helps them gain the confidence to perform it on their own. Please be aware that trial and error is an important part

How to Properly Run Your Activities

Before running an activity that teaches a skill, you should do the following:

- Name the activity.
- Explain the skill you are teaching.
- Position the athletes correctly.
- Explain what the activity will accomplish.
- State the command that will start the activity.
- State the command that will end the activity.

Once you have introduced and repeated the activity a few times in this manner, you will find that merely calling out the name of the activity is sufficient. Your athletes will automatically line up in the proper position to run the activity and practice the skill.

of learning any physical skill. Be patient as athletes make mistakes learning a skill; many wrestling skills can take years to fully master.

Look at the entire skill and then break it down into fundamental components. For example, when teaching a stand-up, your activity sequence could consist of these steps:

1. Getting set in a strong down position
2. Staying strong and upright with one leg up and one knee down
3. Focusing on hand control
4. Coming to the feet and maintaining balance
5. Clearing the opponent's lock and facing him or her

Your teaching duties, though, don't end when all your athletes have demonstrated that they understand how to perform a skill. As you help your athletes improve their skills, your teaching role is in fact just beginning. A significant part of coaching consists of closely observing the hit-and-miss trial performances of your athletes. You will sharpen athletes' skills by detecting errors and correcting them with positive feedback. Your positive feedback will have a great influence on your athletes' motivation to practice and improve their performances. Focus your attention and comments on catching them being good rather than on the inevitable miscues.

Remember, too, that some athletes may need individual instruction. So set aside a time before, during, or after practice to give individual help.

Helping Athletes Improve Skills

After you have successfully taught your athletes the fundamentals of a skill, your focus will be on helping them improve it. Athletes learn skills and improve them at different rates, so don't get frustrated if progress seems slow. Instead, help them progress by shaping their skills and detecting and correcting errors.

Shaping Athletes' Skills

One of your principal teaching duties is to reward positive effort and behavior—in terms of successful skill execution—when you see it. An athlete takes a good shot in practice, and you immediately say, "Good shot! Way to set up your shot and drive through the finish—nice job of staying off your knees." Such comments, plus a smile and a thumbs-up gesture, go a long way toward reinforcing skill technique in that athlete. However, sometimes you may have a long dry spell before you see correct technique to reinforce. It's difficult to reward athletes when they don't execute skills correctly. How can you shape their skills in this case?

Shaping skills takes practice on your athletes' part and patience on yours. Expect them to make errors. Telling the athlete who made the great shot that he or she did a good job doesn't ensure the same success next time. Seeing inconsistency in your athletes' technique can be frustrating. It's even more challenging to stay positive when your athletes repeatedly perform a skill incorrectly or lack enthusiasm for learning. It can be frustrating to see athletes who seemingly don't heed your advice and continue to make the same mistakes.

Please know that it is normal to get frustrated sometimes when teaching skills. Nevertheless, part of successful coaching is controlling this frustration. Instead of getting upset, use these six guidelines for shaping skills:

1. *Think small initially.*

   Reward the first signs of behavior that approximate what you want. Then reward closer and closer approximations of the desired behavior. In short, use your reward power to shape the behavior you seek.

2. *Break skills into small steps.*

   Defending a double-leg takedown attempt, for example, requires a wrestler to be able to use several skills well. A sprawl will get the legs back and the hips down to stretch out the offensive wrestler's arms and will reduce the mechanical advantage. In addition, the defender must block the near side with a whizzer and must also work to keep the attacker's head down, preferably on the mat. If the defender cannot execute each of these skills at the same time, the defense of the double-leg takedown will break down. You will work with your athletes so that they understand how each skill in this technique works together for the full effect and that when all components are strongly executed, the technique will be as well.

3. *Develop one component of a skill at a time.*

Don't try to shape two components of a skill at once. For example, when hitting a switch, athletes must first clear their arm, then move their hips away from their opponent in a side hip-heist. Athletes should focus initially on one aspect (clearing the arm), and then on the other (moving the hips away from the opponent in a side hip-heist). When athletes have problems mastering a skill, it's often because they're trying to improve two or more components at once. Help these athletes to isolate a single component.

However, once the component skills are mastered, be sure to work on the technique as a whole. Each component must be correct, but it may be necessary to actually do two or more things simultaneously. Practicing the technique only as a connected series of independent skills can lead to a sort of lock step performance of the technique.

4. *Use reinforcement occasionally and only for the best examples.*

By focusing only on the best examples, you will help athletes continue to improve once they've mastered the basics. Using occasional reinforcement during practice allows athletes more time to practice skills rather than their having to constantly stop and listen to the coach. Wrestling skills are best learned through repetition, so you need to make the best use of team practice time by allowing the athletes as much time for executing active skills as possible.

5. *Relax your reward standards.*

As athletes focus on mastering a new skill or attempt to integrate it with other skills, their old, well-learned skills may temporarily degenerate, and you may need to relax your expectations. For example, wrestlers who begin to learn a low single may temporarily forget the importance of keeping their head up so they can drive through a double leg properly. Being able to reinforce the importance of that skill with athletes while they learn the low single can reduce the loss of focus on the technique of a double leg.

6. *Go back to the basics.*

If a well-learned skill degenerates for very long, you may need to restore it by going back to the basics. For example, if while working on a single leg, it appears that an athlete has lost the ability to drive through

> **Coaching Tip**
> Introduce self-coaching. With the proper guidance and a positive team environment, athletes who are at least 9 years old can think about how they perform a skill and how they might be able to perform it better. Self-coaching is best done at practice, where an athlete can experiment with learning new skills.

the opponent on a shot, replace work on the single leg with activities that reinforce this skill.

Detecting and Correcting Errors

Good coaches recognize that athletes make two types of errors: learning errors and performance errors. Learning errors are those that occur because athletes don't know how to perform a skill; that is, they have not yet developed the correct motor pattern in the brain to perform a particular skill. Athletes make performance errors not because they don't know how to execute the skill but because they have made a mistake in executing what they do know. There is no easy way to know whether an athlete is making learning or performance errors, and part of the art of coaching is being able to sort out which type of error each mistake is.

The process of helping athletes correct errors begins with your observing and evaluating their performances to determine whether the mistakes are learning or performance errors. Carefully watch your athletes to see whether they routinely make the errors in both practice and match settings, or whether the errors tend to occur only in match settings. If the latter is the case, then your athletes are making performance errors. For performance errors, you need to look for the reasons your athletes are not performing as well as they know how; perhaps they are nervous, or maybe they get distracted by the match setting. If the mistakes are learning errors, then you need to help them learn the skill, which is the focus of this section.

When correcting learning errors, there is no substitute for the coach knowing skills well. The better you understand a skill—not only how one performs it correctly but also what causes learning errors—the more helpful you will be in correcting mistakes.

One of the most common coaching mistakes is to provide inaccurate feedback and advice on how to correct errors. Don't rush into error correction; inaccurate feedback or poor advice will hurt the learning process more than no feedback or instruction at all. If you are uncertain about the cause of the problem or how to correct it, continue to observe and analyze until you are more sure. As a rule, you should see the error repeated several times before attempting to correct it.

Correct One Error at a Time

Suppose Jack, one of your wrestlers, is having trouble with his front head-lock. He's doing most things well, but you notice that he's not scoring as quickly or easily as he should from this position. He gets to the position quickly, and his shoulder is pressuring the center of his opponent's back, and he also has control of his opponent's chin. But often when Jack gets to the front headlock, he loses his footing and drops to his knees, sometimes just to adjust into position but long enough to keep him from getting control of his opponent's near arm. This keeps Jack from being able to get behind quickly for the takedown as his opponent is adjusting to the position. What do you do?

First, decide which error to begin with, because athletes learn more effectively when they attempt to correct one error at a time. Determine whether one error is causing the other; if so, have the athlete correct that error first, because it may eliminate the other error. In Jack's case, dropping to his knees may cause him to miss controlling the near arm, so you should correct the drop to the knees first. When neither error is necessarily causing the other, correct the error that will bring the greatest improvement when remedied, which in turn will likely motivate the athlete to correct the other error.

Use Positive Feedback to Correct Errors

The positive approach to correcting errors includes emphasizing what to do instead of what not to do. Use compliments, praise, rewards, and encouragement to correct errors. Acknowledge correct performance as well as efforts to improve. By using positive feedback, you can help your athletes feel good about themselves and promote a strong desire to achieve.

When you're working with one athlete at a time, the positive approach to correcting errors includes four steps:

1. *Praise effort and proper performance.*

   Praise athletes for trying to perform a skill correctly and for performing any parts of it correctly. Do so immediately after they perform the skill, if possible. Keep the praise simple: "Good try," "Way to stay focused," "Good position," or "That's the way to drive through." You can also use nonverbal feedback like smiling, clapping your hands, or any facial or body expression that shows approval.

   Make sure you're sincere with your praise. Don't indicate that an athlete's efforts are good when they aren't. Athletes usually know whether they have made a sincere effort to perform the skill correctly and perceive undeserved praise for what it is—untruthful feedback to make them feel good. Likewise, don't indicate that an athlete's performance was correct when it wasn't.

2. *Give simple and precise feedback to correct errors.*

   Don't burden an athlete with a long or detailed explanation of how to correct an error. Give just enough feedback that the athlete can correct one error at a time. Before giving feedback, recognize that some athletes readily accept it immediately after the error, whereas others respond better if you delay the correction slightly. Be brief while making your coaching point and get the athlete back into action quickly.

   For errors that are complicated to explain and difficult to correct, try the following:

   • Explain and demonstrate what the athlete should have done. Do not demonstrate what the athlete did wrong.

- Explain the causes of the error if they aren't obvious.
- Explain why you are recommending the correction you have selected if it's not obvious.

3. *Make sure the athlete understands your feedback.*

   If athletes don't understand your feedback, they won't be able to correct an error. Ask athletes to repeat the feedback and to explain and demonstrate how to use it. If they can't do this, be patient and present your feedback again. Then have them repeat the feedback after you're finished.

4. *Provide an environment that motivates the athlete to improve.*

   Your athletes won't always be able to correct their errors immediately, even if they do understand your feedback. Encourage them to hang tough and stick with it when adjustments are difficult or when they seem discouraged. For more difficult corrections, remind them that it will take time, and that the improvement will happen only if they work at it. Encourage athletes who have little self-confidence, by saying something like this: "You were defending against the attacks much better today; with practice you'll be able to block those shots and set up your own attacks." Such support can motivate athletes to continue to refine their skills.

   Some athletes may be self-motivated and need little help from you in this area; with them you can practically ignore step 4 when correcting an error. Although motivation comes from within, try to provide an environment of positive instruction and encouragement to help your athletes improve.

A final note on correcting errors: Although the wrestlers compete as individuals, practices and competitions take place in a team setting. How do you provide individual feedback in a group setting using a positive approach? Instead of yelling across the mat to correct an error (and embarrass the athlete), go to the wrestler or the pair of practice partners. Make the correction quietly and then get the wrestlers back into the activity quickly.

Moving around the room and visiting each athlete or pair of athletes while they work on their skills should be a regular part of your routine. This way, others won't know when you are correcting a pair. This process for feedback has several advantages:

- The wrestler will be more receptive to one-on-one feedback.
- Because the other wrestlers are active and practicing skills, they will be unable to overhear your discussion.
- Because the rest of the team is still working, you'll feel compelled to make your comments simple and concise, which is more helpful to the athlete.

This procedure doesn't mean you can't also use the team setting to give specific, positive feedback. You can do so to reinforce correct group and individual performances. Use this team feedback approach only for positive statements, though. Save corrections for individual discussion.

Dealing With Misbehavior

Children misbehave at times—it's only natural. In coaching situations you have two options for responding to misbehavior: extinction and discipline.

Extinction

Ignoring misbehavior—neither rewarding it nor disciplining it—is called extinction. This approach can be effective under certain circumstances. In some situations, disciplining young people's misbehavior only encourages them to act up further because of the recognition they receive. Ignoring misbehavior teaches youngsters that it is not worth your attention.

Sometimes, though, you cannot wait for a behavior to fizzle out. When athletes endanger themselves or others or disrupt the activities of others, you need to take immediate action. Tell the offending athlete that the behavior must stop and that discipline will follow if it doesn't. If the child doesn't stop misbehaving after the warning, follow through with discipline.

Extinction also doesn't work well when misbehavior is self-rewarding. For example, you may be able to keep from grimacing if a youngster kicks you in the shin, but the kid still knows you were hurt—therein lies the reward. In such circumstances, you must discipline the athlete for the undesirable behavior.

Extinction works best in situations in which athletes are seeking recognition through mischievous behaviors, clowning, or grandstanding. Usually, if you are patient, their failure to get your attention will cause the behavior to disappear. However, be alert so that you don't extinguish desirable behavior. When youngsters do something well, they expect to be positively reinforced. Not rewarding them will likely cause them to discontinue the desired behavior.

Discipline

Some educators say coaches should never discipline young people but should only reinforce their positive behaviors. They argue that discipline does not work, creates hostility, and sometimes leads to avoidance behaviors that may be more unwholesome than the original problem behavior. It is true that discipline does not always work and that it can create problems when used ineffectively, but when used appropriately, discipline is effective in eliminating undesirable behaviors without creating undesirable consequences. You must use discipline effectively, because it is impossible to guide athletes through positive reinforcement and extinction alone. Discipline is part of the positive approach when these guidelines are followed:

- Discipline in a corrective way to help athletes improve now and in the future. Don't discipline to retaliate and make yourself feel better.

- Impose discipline in a matter-of-fact way when athletes break team rules or otherwise misbehave. Shouting at or scolding children indicates that your attitude is one of revenge.

- Once a rule has been agreed on, ensure that athletes who violate it experience the unpleasant consequences of their misbehavior. Warn athletes once before disciplining, but don't wave discipline threateningly over their heads—just do it.

- Be consistent in administering discipline.

- Don't discipline using consequences that may cause you guilt. If you can't think of an appropriate consequence right away, tell athletes you will talk with them after you think about it. You might consider involving athletes in designing a consequence.

- Once the discipline is completed, don't make athletes feel that they are in the doghouse. Always let them know that they're valued members of the team.

- Make sure that what you think is discipline isn't perceived by the athlete as a positive reinforcement. For instance, keeping an athlete out of a certain activity or portion of the training session may be just what the child desired.

- Never discipline athletes for making errors when they are competing.

- Never use physical activity—running laps or doing push-ups—as discipline. To do so only causes athletes to resent physical activity, and you want them to learn to enjoy it throughout their lives.

- Discipline sparingly. Constant discipline and criticism cause athletes to resent you and to turn their interests elsewhere as well.

7

Developing the Seven Basic Skills

Wrestling *on the feet*, also known as the neutral position, is the starting point for teaching wrestling skills. Wrestlers must be fundamentally sound on their feet, on offense and defense, to be successful. Sound technique on the feet leads to takedowns that score points and put the top wrestler in a strong position that the opponent must work hard to overcome. Wrestlers who score the first takedown win a high percentage of matches.

To wrestle effectively on their feet, your wrestlers must learn the following seven basic skills:

1. Position
2. Motion
3. Changing levels
4. Penetration
5. Lifting
6. Back step
7. Back arch

To score a takedown, wrestlers need to establish a solid stance *(position)*, be able to move in any direction without exposing themselves while creating angles for their own attack *(motion)*, be able to move up or down so they can attack above or below the opponent's center of gravity *(changing levels)*, and be able to move through the opponent *(penetration)*. Many takedown techniques require the ability to effectively lift the opponent *(lifting)*. More advanced techniques require the agility to make quick pivots that generate torque *(back step)* and the agility to fall back in an arched position while passing the opponent's body over the top and onto the mat into a danger position *(back arch)*.

As you teach these seven basic skills, remember to use the IDEA approach to teaching skills—introduce, demonstrate, and explain the skill, and attend to wrestlers as they practice the skill. For a refresher on IDEA, see chapter 6. If you aren't familiar with wrestling skills, rent or purchase a video to see the skills performed. In addition, please note that we provide information about only the basics of wrestling in this book. As your wrestlers advance in their skills, you'll need to advance in your knowledge as a coach. You can do so by learning from your experiences, by watching and talking with more experienced coaches, and by studying advanced resources. Many such resources are available from USA Wrestling and the American Sport Education Program. Coaches and wrestlers can learn a tremendous amount by watching great wrestlers. If there are college teams or consistently good high school programs in your area, attend their competitions, ask coaches and wrestlers questions, and attend their clinics and camps.

Position

To start a match, both wrestlers are on their feet in the neutral position, and each wrestler has one foot on his or her line near the center of the mat (see figure 7.1) so that the wrestlers are close to each other when the action begins. When the official blows the whistle to signal the start of the action, both competitors must be in good position to attack as well as defend against the

Creating Opportunities Using Setups

Setups are the tactics that wrestlers use to create advantageous situations in which they can use their technical skills most effectively. To score a takedown, for example, a wrestler would first use a specific tactic to create an advantage, a *setup*. After the setup, the wrestler can perform the takedown technique. The concept of a setup is used in other sports as well. For example, a boxer must use a jab with the left hand to set up the right hand, where his or her power lies. Otherwise the boxer would never be able to land a knockout punch cleanly. A baseball pitcher may have a dominant 100-mile-per-hour fastball, but he can't throw it every time because eventually the batters will learn what is coming and simply start the swing earlier. Instead, almost all pitchers use a variety of pitches (curveball, slider, changeup, and so on) in order to keep the batter guessing. Likewise a wrestler cannot just walk up to a skilled opponent, grab the legs, and take him or her to the ground. Instead, the wrestler would likely use a setup such as a fake attack, manipulation of momentum, or misdirection in order to get past an aware defender. Simply stated, setups create opportunities.

Setups can be thought of as an *if, then, else* statement. The opponent is in great position and moves well, so the wrestler must do something to counteract that. *If* the defender doesn't react, *then* the attacker tries something *else* and moves on to another setup and attack. Of course, the opponent is working though the same scenario, which is what makes wrestling such a great sport.

As your wrestlers learn the seven basic skills, they also need to learn about setups. When they learn to make their opponents take a step to a specific spot by establishing a good position inside the arms and moving the defender with their own motion, they can then anticipate where the leg they hope to attack will land even before changing their level, and the element of surprise will become an advantage.

opponent's attack. Proper body position—the ability of a wrestler to control specific parts of the body in relation to each other—is the first requirement for successful execution of any takedown or countermaneuver. Positioned properly, a wrestler will be able to move freely in any direction without making awkward movements that may encourage the opponent's attack. Proper position has to do with the relationship between body parts and the center of gravity, the hips. The objective of most attacks is to get under the opponent's center of gravity; therefore, it is equally important that wrestlers keep their own center of gravity comfortably low. If it is too low, however, movement will be restricted; on the other hand, if it is too high, the chance of a possible attack increases.

To assume the proper neutral position, a wrestler should place the feet approximately shoulder-width apart to provide both a wide base of support for stability and good balance for quick motion, then drop the hips by flexing the knees. In the neutral position, a wrestler should face the opponent directly,

Figure 7.1   Starting a match in the neutral position.

always trying to keep the shoulders square with the opponent. The wrestler may face the opponent in a square stance, with the toes of both feet aligned with the body and the chest, as shown in figure 7.2a, or the wrestler may face the opponent in a staggered stance, with one foot in front of the other, as shown in figure 7.2b. A wrestler's stance is generally a matter of comfort, so as a coach you should teach both stances and let the wrestler decide which is more comfortable. Both wrestlers should be in a good position, and both should be working to stay squared to the opponent (see figure 7.3). If one wrestler can effectively use movement to create an angle, it will provide a position of advantage for an attack.

As mentioned previously, wrestlers who are able to maintain a strong, athletic, neutral stance are more likely to succeed in attacking an opponent

a   b

Figure 7.2   Neutral position: (a) square stance and (b) staggered stance.

and defending an opponent's attack because they will be able to move freely in any direction and be ready to change levels and penetrate explosively, or they will be able to change levels and sprawl powerfully. In either the square or staggered stance, the wrestler must learn how to maintain the proper position and relationship of body parts as described in figure 7.4.

Figure 7.3   Wrestlers maintaining a square position in relation to each other.

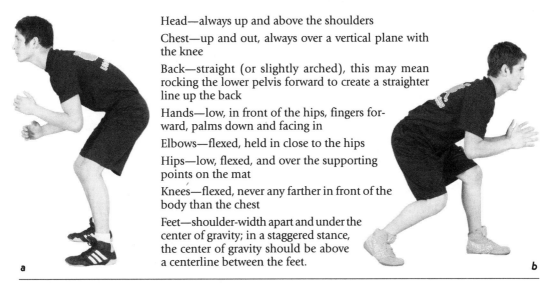

Head—always up and above the shoulders

Chest—up and out, always over a vertical plane with the knee

Back—straight (or slightly arched), this may mean rocking the lower pelvis forward to create a straighter line up the back

Hands—low, in front of the hips, fingers forward, palms down and facing in

Elbows—flexed, held in close to the hips

Hips—low, flexed, and over the supporting points on the mat

Knees—flexed, never any farther in front of the body than the chest

Feet—shoulder-width apart and under the center of gravity; in a staggered stance, the center of gravity should be above a centerline between the feet.

a

b

Figure 7.4   Proper position and relationship of the body in the *(a)* square stance and *(b)* staggered stance.

Motion

A wrestler's motion should be fluid and relaxed because when the body is in good position and the muscles are relaxed, motion can be generated more quickly. Further, proper position and relaxed, smooth motion make the wrestler less susceptible to the opponent's setup attempts. Pulling, pushing, or snapping the head of a wrestler in proper position who is moving smoothly will not produce as much of a reaction as when the wrestler is in a rigid, tight stance.

If your wrestlers are in a good stance and are prepared to move well, they will be in position to make sound attacks and to avoid an opponent's attack. When teaching motion, first instruct wrestlers to circle an opponent, maintaining a good stance, and move into or away from an opponent at angles. Moving straight in, or backing straight out, can make the wrestler vulnerable to an attack. If a wrestler moves straight at an opponent, the opponent will know exactly where to aim at the body, such as a leg. If a wrestler backs up directly, he or she is typically shifting the weight onto the heels and compromises balance. Wrestlers also can be penalized for backing up too much, either for stalling or fleeing the mat. A wrestler should move the feet smoothly in quick, short steps, making sure the feet don't cross.

Coach your wrestlers to watch their opponent's movement. If the opponent crosses the feet while moving, the wrestler should be ready to attack just as the feet cross because the opponent will not be able to react quickly from that position. If the opponent moves the feet in a predictable pattern, timing the steps and making an attack just as a foot is planted is a great tactic. If your wrestler sees that an opponent is about to shift to the right and plant a foot there, your wrestler knows that the opponent's weight will be centered on that foot at least momentarily as it lands and he or she pushes off from that foot to move again. While the opponent's weight is centered on that foot, he or she cannot quickly move that leg to avoid your wrestler's attack.

Changing Levels

When effective motion has put a wrestler in position to make an attack, especially a leg attack, changing levels is important. First, a level change positions the attacker's center of gravity below the defender's. The center of gravity is where the core of each wrestler's strength is, and the wrestler who attacks right at the strongest spot is not likely to succeed. Second, the level change puts the attacking wrestler's strongest muscles, the legs and hips, in the loaded position. For example, envision an archer drawing a bow to the firing position, or even a coiled spring. The hips and legs are now like the drawn bow or the spring, ready to explode and penetrate through the opponent.

To change levels, the wrestler must first be in a strong stance, as shown in figure 7.5a, with the head up. The wrestler wants to be as close to the opponent as possible when beginning to change levels. This is because an aware opponent will start moving away as soon as he or she senses what is happening. If the wrestler is too far away when starting the process, the opponent's leg will be out of reach. The wrestler should step back with the right foot, then drop the hips, changing levels to end up in the *loaded* position, ready to drive forward with the right leg while making the penetration step with the

Figure 7.5 Changing levels.

left. This is true no matter whether the wrestler starts in a square or staggered stance. The resulting position looks similar to a staggered stance, but the wrestler's hips are lowered six inches or more from their regular stance, the feet are closer together, and the wrestler has dropped the hips enough that the hands can touch the mat (see figure 7.5b). Now the wrestler should be as close to the opponent as possible so that making a penetration step and driving onto the lead knee moves him or her through the opponent's hips (see "Penetration" below).

In wrestling, many positions are not instinctive and will not be comfortable right away. Changing levels to get under the opponent's center of gravity will most likely be one of those positions for your young wrestlers. It might feel right to your wrestlers to penetrate from their basic neutral stance without changing levels. However, trying to go from that relatively high position to a double- or single-leg attack puts their forward movement at an angle that could in turn take them right into the mat if the opponent were to step back.

Penetration

When proper position and effective movement have put your wrestler close to the opponent at the proper angle, and the level change has been

Coaching Tip
Teach your wrestlers to stay loose in their stance. If wrestlers are tense, they must overcome that before being able to make an explosive move of any sort. You may find that this is a difficult task for beginners who are trying hard to keep all of the positioning cues in mind. One way to encourage staying loose is to have your wrestlers practice circling in one direction or moving side to side in a continuous motion. (Wrestlers typically don't move straight in or straight out.) While standing still, it is easy for a wrestler to become locked into a firm stance, providing a fixed target for the opponent. By staying in motion, wrestlers prevent themselves from locking up and also keep their opponent from knowing where to aim (in a sense throwing a curveball instead of the expected fastball).

made, penetration is next. When wrestlers penetrate, they move past or through the opponent's defenses, namely the hands and arms, transferring their own weight onto the opponent and then transferring their combined mass onto the opponent's legs, feet, and heels. The defender will not be able to retreat as fast as the attacker can penetrate. As the wrestler continues to penetrate through the opponent's space, the opponent will lose control of his or her position and maybe even go all the way to the mat.

To penetrate an opponent and initiate a takedown, a wrestler needs to be in a good stance with a low center of gravity. The wrestler then takes a penetration step toward—or just past—the opponent's feet to move the opponent into a vulnerable position. The penetration should be directed at the opponent's center of gravity—the hips. Simply stated, penetration is moving to and through the opponent by driving through the opponent's hips. For example, your wrestler can take a penetration step with the right foot, planting it just past the opponent's left foot (see figure 7.6a), or vice versa. Now the wrestler is in a close position to attempt a takedown (see figure 7.6b).

Remind your wrestlers that their center of gravity is below their opponent's and that penetrating with power from a strong position minimizes the risk of a counterattack. A crucial aspect of penetration is power, but power is sometimes not well understood. If wrestlers have strength, they can pick up the opponent. If they have endurance and strength, they can do it many times. But power involves moving a mass over a distance with speed. The basic goal of explosive penetration is to get the attacker's mass moving though the defender so quickly that the opponent cannot react well. If a wrestler can use motion to create an angle for attack and then smoothly change levels and use explosive power to penetrate through the opponent's center of gravity, the wrestler will have a great chance to score.

a   b

Figure 7.6   Penetrating an opponent.

Lifting

Lifting is used in several situations, namely during takedown techniques and while countering escape attempts. A wrestler can lift from several positions, including upright neutral, upright while controlling from behind, and from the top riding position. Proper technique applies to any position. Wrestlers lift primarily with their biggest muscles—the hips and legs. Although the arms and hands do have a role, many young wrestlers place too much emphasis on the upper body. This can put too much stress on the back and doesn't take advantage of the wrestler's true power.

When first teaching lifting, have your wrestlers lock their arms and hands around a partner's waist from behind, from the side, or at an angle, depending on the situation. With the head behind the opponent, wrestler's should firmly hug their opponent's body to their own (see figure 7.7). Young wrestlers can make themselves stronger by shortening their grip into a butterfly lock (see figure 7.8). This removes the flexible hands and wrists from the equation as much as possible, and if fewer points can flex or be attacked by the defender, the wrestler's effective strength will be magnified.

After locking the arms and hands around the opponent and securing the opponent to the body, the wrestler steps in closer so that the feet are at least level with the opponent's. Next, the wrestler lowers his or her body until the hips are below the partner's (see figure 7.9a). This enables the wrestler to lift using the power of the legs. Picture a loaded spring ready to open and pop upward forcefully. Holding the partner tightly to his or her body, the wrestler locks the opponent's hips in position above his or her own. (Think about how you would lift and carry a heavy box—you would want your center of gravity under that of the box, and you would hold the box close to your body.) Now

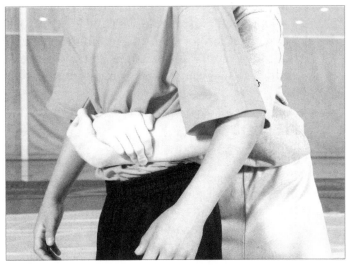

Figure 7.7 Securing the opponent to the body for a lift.

Figure 7.8 Butterfly lock.

Figure 7.9   Lifting an opponent.

the wrestler just has to straighten the legs (think of the spring), driving the hips forward and up (see figure 7.9*b*), and the opponent will come off the mat.

Monitor all wrestlers as they learn to lift, especially your beginning and younger wrestlers. Their goal should be to leave no space between themselves and the partner's hips before lifting. This point becomes more important as the wrestlers move into competitive situations. The wrestler trying to escape in this situation needs to create space between his or her hips and the top wrestler. Conversely, the top wrestler must try to prevent space from developing so that he or she can lift effectively and return the opponent to the mat. In addition, teach your young wrestlers that they have an obligation to bring their opponent to the mat under control and safely. Although this is the right thing to do, there are penalties that can lead to disqualification for slamming the opponent so forcefully or out of control that the opponent becomes injured and cannot continue within the injury time limit. That said, wrestling is a contact sport, and wrestlers can return their opponents to the mat firmly enough to make an impression without hurting them.

Back Step

The back step is a skill used in several takedown situations. It generates force in a compact space using hip rotation, and the power increases as the speed of the force, or torque, increases. A wrestler who can skillfully execute a smooth, fast back step can increase strength dramatically. The back step is used most often to initiate techniques such as the headlock and hip toss. It can be used as a low technique in which the attacker follows through by rolling onto the outside knee and then the hips. It can also be used as a higher technique in which the move is finished by rapidly lifting the hips as a throw is completed. This may be more spectacular, but it provides less control.

The back step normally starts from a position where both wrestlers are tied up. To set up a back step to the left, the attacker should grasp the opponent's right arm below the elbow with the left hand (see figure 7.10*a*). The attacker's right arm can be wrapped around the defender's back, up in the armpit as an underhook, over the opponent's left arm as an overhook, or it could be tied up on the opponent's neck and head. The location is unimportant, but the wrestler needs to establish a second point of upper-body control (in figure 7.10*a*, the attacker's right arm is in an underhook).

During a hip toss, the back step to the left starts with the attacker stepping with the right foot to a spot just in front of the defender's own right foot (see figure 7.10*b*). The attacker must then lower his or her level a small amount and rotate the hips counterclockwise, stepping the left foot to the right so that the toes of the left foot are about at the heel of the right—the back step (see figure 7.10*c*). This should bring the attacker's hips all the way through, passing in front of the opponent's hips. A back step to the right is done in the same way, using the opposite side of the body.

Figure 7.10   Executing a back step to the left during a hip toss.

Back Arch

Think of the back arch as an extension of lifting; many of the elements are similar. The wrestler has some sort of lock on the opponent: a body lock, both arms locked around the opponent's chest with an arm trapped, or an over-and-under in which one arm is over and one arm under the opponent's. The back arch starts the same as the basic lift: by stepping into the opponent and changing levels to get the hips below the defender's. Again, just as in the basic lift, the role of the arms is to keep the opponent's body locked to the attacker's. Thus, the defender's body has to go where the attacker's does. With the attacker holding the bodies tightly together, making the level change, and stepping in so that his or her hips are under the defender's (see figure 7.11a), the attacker completes the back arch by falling back and explosively driving the hips up into the defender's center of gravity by extending the legs. As the defender's body starts to pass over the top and forward, the attacker twists the body, which twists the defender's (see figure 7.11b), and they land with the defender in a near fall position and the attacker on top. This can be drilled effectively with a dummy until young wrestlers feel comfortable with the sensation of lifting and arching.

If your young wrestlers can learn to do the back arch well, it will open up many other techniques to them as they advance in their knowledge, particularly if they want to also wrestle freestyle and Greco-Roman.

Figure 7.11 Back arch.

Young wrestlers and new coaches who watch the very best wrestlers may think that these wrestlers execute a variety of spectacular techniques that they could never learn or teach. However, the best wrestlers simply put these seven basic skills together more consistently than others. They know that although it seems like it creates too many time-consuming steps, taking the time to use effective motion, to change levels, and to penetrate gets better results more quickly than diving in from a position that is too high does. Diving in too quickly often results in an unnecessary struggle that may score, but only after using up too much time and energy.

The great John Smith may be the best example we have of combining the seven basic skills—Smith chained movements together effectively. Knowing the reaction that each would produce from the opponent, Smith often changed levels to initiate a low single leg way before the opponent was stepping to the place Smith knew the foot and leg would be. He was startlingly fast, no doubt. However, using just these basic skills, he was not only fast but also effective. Recordings at normal speed of Smith against even his toughest opponents show breathtaking takedowns. Watching the same action in slow motion, you can see exactly how Smith employs the seven basic skills and how, chained together, these basic skills produce spectacular results.

8

Coaching Attacks and Counterattacks

When wrestling on the feet, both wrestlers look for opportunities to initiate an attack, and at the same time both must be aware of potential attacks by their opponent. A case can easily be made for the idea that "the best defense is a good offense." It is true that constant work to set up and execute takedowns may pressure opponents so much that they will have trouble generating an offense of their own. A case can also be made that the best offense comes from a good defense. In reality, both can be true.

Many great wrestlers have separated themselves from their competition because they are simply difficult to score against. If your wrestlers are able to maintain great position, move well, use their hands well, and control the head position, it will be difficult for opponents to score on them. Interestingly, these defensive skills are the same skills needed to initiate many attacks.

You and your wrestlers should work together to help them develop discipline on the feet. When opponents are unable get your wrestlers out of their game plan, frustration sets in for the opponent. This normally results in the opponent taking more chances, which equals more scoring opportunities for your wrestlers.

Tie-Ups

Wrestlers use tie-ups to control opponents and move them into positions that open up takedown opportunities. When wrestlers are attempting to tie up, they are competing for control of the situation, which they gain by grasping the opponent's upper body in one of several ways:

- Underhook—A wrestler slides an arm between the torso and upper arm of the opponent, raising the hand and effectively "hooking" the elbow under the armpit (see figure 8.1*a*).

- Overhook—A wrestler wraps an arm around the back of the opponent's upper arm and slides the hand between the torso and upper arm so that the hand rests between his or her own chest and the opponent's chest (see figure 8.1*b*).

- Head tie—A wrestler places the forearm on the collarbone of the opponent and grasps the back of the opponent's head or neck with the hand (see figure 8.1*c*).

These positions, when used correctly, allow a wrestler to control the movement and balance of an opponent. Young wrestlers should work hard on several concepts that will make their tie-ups more effective.

Having a Purpose

Teach your wrestlers to initiate contact for a tie-up only when they know exactly why they are doing it. Most offense is initiated by using contact to

Figure 8.1   Tie-ups: *(a)* underhook, *(b)* overhook, and *(c)* head tie.

create opportunities to exploit an opponent's defense (see the discussion of setups in chapter 7). Therefore, a wrestler creating contact without a purpose allows the opponent to use the contact to create his or her *own* opportunity. This is why a wrestler who does not intend to use contact to create an opportunity is usually better served by maintaining proper position and staying in motion at a safe distance.

Maintaining a Strong Head Position

During tie-ups, head position is the key to both offense and defense. If your wrestlers have the head up and are in a good stance, it is more difficult for their opponents to move them around with tie-ups on the head. If your wrestlers have the head down and are facing the mat, it is fairly easy for the opponent to tie up on the head to initiate several offensive techniques. The same is true for opponents—if the head is up, your wrestlers will have to rely on smart movement to create angles because it will be more difficult to move the opponent into position for an attack.

Strong head position will make your wrestlers better both offensively and defensively. Coach your wrestlers to maintain disciplined head positions. Instead of being tied up in an ear-to-ear position, as shown in figure 8.2, work with them to dictate control of the situation by forcing the opponent to be forehead to forehead (see figure 8.3*a*), forehead to temple (see figure 8.3*b*), or even forehead to the side of the opponent's neck (see figure 8.3*c*). If your wrestlers can do this, they will be in a position of advantage—they have the angle for initiating an attack, and the opponent has given up head position, which is a huge disadvantage.

Ties, such as the collar tie, that result in an ear-to-ear position are not very productive. In the collar tie, both wrestler's heads are in contact, and each wrestler uses the same hand and arm to tie up by grasping the other's neck—at the collar. That is, either the right or left arm is on the head, and each uses the free arm to grasp the elbow of the arm tied up on the neck. If they both attempt to pull each other in tight, their heads end up ear to ear, and it is difficult for either to score. On the other hand, if your youth wrestlers force their opponents to stay forehead to forehead, your wrestlers will be in a better position offensively. Most opponents find it impossible to make a successful takedown attempt if they cannot successfully move past a wrestler's head. If your wrestler works to maintain forehead-to-forehead contact (or even just close) with an opponent using this solid head position, your wrestler will be able to change levels with the opponent and make it extremely difficult for the opponent to complete the move.

If your wrestler is in the opponent's tie-up on the head, aggressively working to keep the head up gives the opponent less neck to control. In practice, have your wrestlers get in their stance and feel what happens to the back of

Figure 8.2 Ear-to-ear head position for a tie-up makes it more difficult to generate offense.

Figure 8.3   Correct head positions for a tie-up: *(a)* forehead to forehead, *(b)* forehead to temple, and *(c)* forehead to neck.

their neck if they work at keeping their head up compared to looking slightly downward. Have them place their own hand flat on the back of their own neck, then look down and then move their head back into good position. It is difficult for the opponent to control your wrestler's neck when the head position is correct.

Maintaining Movement

Wrestlers must maintain movement when using tie-ups because there is no point in tying up an opponent and then standing still. Tie-ups are used to move the opponent into position to initiate takedown attempts. Just as in other wrestling situations, the arms play a part, but not the major role, in the movement. Rather, they bring the opponent into the position your wrestlers want the opponent to be in before making an attack. Your wrestlers may be tied up with an opponent and want to make a single-leg attempt to the right. By circling to the left, with an inside-arm tie or head tie on the opponent's left side, they will force the defender to step forward with the left leg. As your wrestlers develop a feel for this and figure out the timing, they will learn that they can start making their level change and penetration step just as the opponent's leg starts to come toward them. If your wrestlers arrive at the leg just as the foot hits the mat, it is difficult for the defender to overcome this disadvantage. Different movements produce different reactions, but no movement produces no action!

Achieving Inside Control

In tie-up situations, the wrestler with the most inside control is in the stronger position. The inside wrestler no longer has to figure out how to get through the first line of defense—the hands and arms—and the other wrestler does. If your wrestler is controlling the elbow of the arm in the head tie and has an inside tie-up on the other arm—done by reaching from the inside above the elbow and wrapping the hand around to grasp the triceps—it may look like the wrestler with the head tie is in control, but your wrestler really is in the stronger position.

One High, One Low   Moving on from this start, if the opponent initiates a tie-up, there is no need to mirror it. It can be as effective to tie up that elbow and the opponent's free wrist. Similarly, when your wrestlers choose to make a tie-up on the other wrestler's neck, they should keep the other hand low, tying up the free wrist or arm at the elbow. If both are high, they are susceptible to some takedown techniques.

Thumb on the Outside   When opponents tie up on your wrestler's head, coach them to automatically control that elbow by grasping the arm just above the elbow with the thumb on the outside. The wrester does not have to, but if he or she can control the opponent's far wrist, your wrestler is in an even stronger position. With the head up and in good position—forehead to forehead or your wrestler's forehead to the opponent's temple, and with the thumb on the outside—your wrestler will be able to execute several offensive techniques and also will be in position to control the action so that the opponent cannot attack.

Attacks

There are three levels of attacks: high-level attacks from the waist to the head, midlevel attacks from the knees to the waist, and low-level attacks from the knees down. Youth wrestlers do not need to know a lot of techniques and can be successful knowing just a couple of techniques for each level very well.

High-Level Attacks

The most common high-level attacks in youth folkstyle wrestling are headlocks and elbow shucks.

Headlocks

Headlocks are holds in which the attacking wrestler's arms are locked around the defender's neck and one arm. There are three basic applications of the headlock: the basic headlock, the reverse headlock, and the elbow shuck.

Basic Headlock   The basic headlock is initiated from a tie-up situation, as previously discussed in "Tie-Ups." Your wrestler must secure a tie-up with his or her forehead on the opponent's temple and an inside tie-up on the far arm, grasping the triceps. On the near side, the offensive wrestler must secure one of the following tie-ups: a head tie, an overhook on the near arm, or an inside tie on the near arm.

Wrestlers can use any of these three tie-ups as they get ready to initiate a basic headlock. When using an inside tie or overhook, wrestlers move the near arm toward the head. Wrestlers might choose a head tie because the arm is already near the head, but this tie gives up the element of surprise a bit. Your wrestlers need to end up with the near arm coming over the top of the back of the opponent's neck, and these positions are starting points for initiating the technique. For example, it would be difficult for a wrestler to bring the near hand all the way up from the hip and go right into a headlock because the opponent would have ample time to react.

Your wrestler should simultaneously pull down with the far arm while releasing the tie-up (an overhook in this example) and forcefully wrap the other around the opponent's neck (see figure 8.4*a*). The wrestler should then step across to near the opponent's far foot with the foot on the same side as the arm on the neck and drop the hips a bit and step back to powerfully rotate the hips through between the two wrestlers' bodies (see figures 8.4*b* and 8.4*c*). Your wrestler then whips the head and arm over and toward the mat, while simultaneously "sagging" the entire body down to the mat, and rolling onto the hip (see figure 8.4*d*). In this position, with the opponent on his or her back, your wrestler gets the hands in a butterfly lock, as discussed in chapter 7, if he or she has not already done so during the throw, and moves the hips away from the opponent so that the two bodies form a 90-degree angle. This makes it difficult for the defender to roll the attacker through and reverse the positions. Your wrestler should then cinch up the headlock as tight as possible with the ribs on the opponent's chest and the hips off the mat so that the defender carries as much of the weight as possible. Encourage your wrestler to be patient, feel what the defender is trying to do, and vary the weight on the body and leverage on the head and arm to work the shoulder blades to the mat for the fall.

Reverse Headlock   The reverse headlock is just that, the reverse of the basic headlock. It can be effective for young wrestlers because it happens when the opponent is in what seems to be a secure position, and it takes the opponent forcefully to his or her back. Because the reverse headlock is set up when the opponent resists going with a regular headlock, the two can be used together.

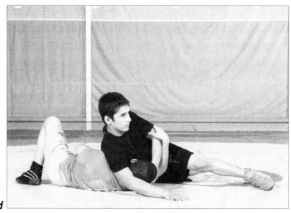

Figure 8.4   Basic headlock.

Coaching Tip

When working on the reverse headlock with any wrestlers, and especially your youth wrestlers, encourage them to keep their opponent's safety in mind. It can be tempting for inexperienced wrestlers to try to stop this throw by placing their free hand on the mat. If the throw happens correctly, this can bring the combined weight of both wrestlers onto that arm and may cause injury.

Again, like the basic headlock, the reverse headlock begins with the wrestlers in a tie-up. Your wrestler must initiate a tie-up with his or her forehead on the opponent's temple and an underhook on the same side by reaching through the opponent's armpit and wrapping the hand over the top of the shoulder from behind and with the free hand, tying up on the neck.

From the underhook tie-up, your wrestler should now work to get his or her hands locked around the opponent's head and near arm (see figure 8.5a), shortening up the grip as much as possible using a butterfly lock and driving the elbows toward each other, "pinching" and further tightening the headlock (see figure 8.5b). Your wrestler steps in with the leg on the underhook side, so that his or her hip is in front of the defender's (see figure 8.5c), and while driving the

Figure 8.5   Reverse headlock.

arm and head over to the mat, your wrestler changes levels (see figure 8.5d). Your wrestler then turns to face away from the opponent and forcefully drives the leg that had been stepped in straight back between the opponent's legs. When the wrestlers hit the mat they will be chest to chest (see figure 8.5e), with the opponent in a near fall position Like in the basic headlock, your wrestler should again work to get 90 degrees to the opponent, keeping his or her weight on the opponent.

Elbow Shuck   An elbow shuck is an effective takedown technique when the opponent has your wrestler tied up on the head. For example, consider that the opponent has a grip on your wrestler's neck with the right hand (see figure 8.6a). In this situation, first coach your wrestlers to keep the head up and to maintain good head position—forehead to forehead, or forehead to temple on the tie-up side—to prevent the opponent from controlling your wrestler's neck. Your wrestler should then grasp the opponent's elbow on the tie-up arm, with the thumb on the outside. In this example, your wrestler will

Figure 8.6 Elbow shuck.

use the left hand to grasp the opponent's right elbow (see figure 8.6b) and will get a tie-up on the inside or wrist of the opponent's opposite arm using the right hand (see figure 8.6c).

Next, your wrestler circles into the opponent, toward the arm on the neck (see figure 8.6d). When your wrestler gets an angle on the tie-up side, he or she initiates the elbow shuck by driving the opponent's elbow straight at the opposite pectoral, keeping the head up and following the elbow in (see figure 8.6e).

This elbow shuck can be finished in several ways:

- *High-level, go-behind move.* When releasing the opponent's far arm, your wrestler can choose to finish this higher by reaching across the defender's body to grab at the far hip (see figure 8.7a). As the opponent is driven onto the heels by the elbow shuck, your wrestler can then step behind with the outside leg and lock hands around the defender's waist to lift and return the defender to the mat (see figure 8.7b).

- *Midlevel single leg or tackle.* As the opponent's hand comes off the head, your wrestler can change levels and penetrate explosively, attacking the near leg at the angle that has been created, taking a full penetration step and picking up the single leg (see figure 8.8). This is discussed in the following section on midlevel attacks. Occasionally, the reaction drives the opponent onto the heels so much that this can be finished as a more simple tackle, as shown in figure 8.9.

Figure 8.7   High-level finish for the elbow shuck.

Figure 8.8   Midlevel single-leg finish for the elbow shuck.

Figure 8.9   Tackle finish for the elbow shuck.

Midlevel Attacks

The most common midlevel attacks in youth folkstyle wrestling are the single leg, double leg, and high crotch.

Single Leg

There are many ways to execute a takedown by grasping one leg—called the *single leg*. Regardless of the setup used for the single leg, teach your young wrestlers to first move themselves or their opponent or both so that they have an angle to attack from (see figure 8.10*a*). As discussed in chapter 7, gaining an angle provides several advantages. Attacking from an angle takes your wrestler's attack across the powerful center of the defender's body, rather than directly into it. Also, the defender's sprawl—dropping the hips and thrusting the legs back—is much less effective if your wrestler attacks at an angle.

a

b

c

Figure 8.10   Single leg.

Next, your wrestler should change levels and make an inside penetration step that ends up with the head positioned against the opponent's chest (see figure 8.10b). The step should be deep enough that when your wrestler drives forward onto the inside knee, his or her weight moves all the way through the space the defender was in. While penetrating, your wrestler should grasp the single leg with both arms straight, locked behind the knee, and step up with the outside leg first and then the inside (see figure 8.10c).

From this position, there a several ways to finish. The one your wrestlers should use depends on what the defender does.

- When your wrestler has a leg up and the head on the opponent's chest and the opponent defends with a whizzer, your wrestler should execute a technique called *running the pipe*. While pushing down on the defender's thigh with the chest and into the opponent with the head, the attacker should pull up with the arms as hard as possible, making a powerful lever (see figure 8.11). When teaching this, have your wrestlers watch the defender's foot. When the pressure is correct, they will be able to see the foot being pushed into the mat.

- If the defender is trying to use a whizzer by driving an arm between your wrestler's outside arm and body and levering as hard as possible, the defender's pressure plus your wrestler's pressure make the defender vulnerable. Your wrestler can step across with the inside foot over to the defender's foot on the mat (see figure 8.12a). Next, your wrestler can step back and change levels by forcefully dropping, pulling the leg through between the attacker's own, and continuing the downward pressure with the upper body (see figure 8.12b).

- If there is no whizzer, your wrestler can quickly drive into the defender (see figure 8.13a), creating enough space to step the inside leg over and outside of the single leg to clear it (see figure 8.13b) and then lift the single leg straight up into the armpit (see figure 8.13c). Teach

Figure 8.11   Running the pipe.

Figure 8.12 Using a back step to complete a single-leg takedown when the defender uses a whizzer.

Figure 8.13 Completing the single-leg takedown when the defender does not use a whizzer.

your wrestlers to keep moving in these situations in order to keep the defender thinking about having to avoid tripping instead of trying to counterattack. They should try to get the defender hopping around and time their move so that just as the defender hops up, they can sweep his or her foot with their outside leg (see figure 8.13*d*), bringing the opponent to the mat (see figure 8.13*e*).

Double Leg

Using a double leg simply means that a wrestler attacks both legs. The double leg is effective against an opponent who is in a square stance because both legs are equally close to the attacker. It may be initiated straight on or from an angle. If a wrestler is not able to get an effective angle for a single leg, he or she might want to initiate a double-leg attack from straight on. A double leg could also be more effective against wrestlers who are highly skilled in defending single-leg attacks. To return to the baseball analogy from chapter 7, a good pitcher doesn't have just a fastball. Even if he can throw it 100 miles per hour, he still needs a curveball and slider, depending on the batter he is facing.

Your wrestler can use a tie-up, as discussed in "Tie-Ups" on pages 82 through 86, to get through the defender's arms and must use good movement so that he or she can initiate the attack from an angle. Then, when your wrestler is close and has the opponent's arms neutralized, he or she should automatically change levels and start the penetration step (see figure 8.14*a*). The step should go right at the defender, with the foot landing between the feet (see figure 8.14*b*). As your wrestler drives forward onto the knee, the head must stay up and outside the body. With good penetration and follow-through, the outside leg steps up, and the arms should wrap at the knees (see figure 8.14*c*).

There are several ways to finish a double-leg takedown:

- If your wrestler has deep penetration and the opponent is caught on his or her heels, your wrestler can drive straight through and send the opponent to his or her back (see figure 8.15).

- Your wrestler can use a penetration step, step up with the outside leg after the penetration step, lift with the near arm, and pull in with the far arm to collapse the knee (see figure 8.16*a*). Your wrestler drives to that side to finish the takedown. The opponent will either land on a hip or turn facedown as he or she goes down (see figure 8.16*b*).

- If your wrestler's hips are in close enough, he or she can lift the defender off his or her feet and finish to the mat easily from that point. If this is the case, straightening the legs will bring the opponent right off the mat. However, if the defender is able to sprawl at all, it may be tough to finish this way. Ideally, if the defender is leaning over the top of the attacker (the defender's center of gravity resting above the attacker's hips and shoulders) and the attacker's legs are loaded (bent), as shown in figure 8.17*a*, the attacker can stand up with the opponent over his or her shoulder (see figure 8.17*b*). But, if the opponent has sprawled back,

Figure 8.14 Double-leg takedown.

Figure 8.15 Completing the double-leg takedown by driving straight through the defender.

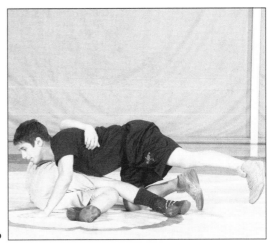

Figure 8.16   Completing the double-leg takedown by using a penetration step.

Figure 8.17   Completing a double-leg takedown by taking the defender off of his feet.

the opponent's center of gravity will be spread in front of the attacker. This creates leverage and makes it more difficult for your wrestler to lift the opponent. Remind wrestlers to think of picking up a box or other heavy object. If they hold it tight to the torso, it is much easier to lift than if they try to pick it up while it is two feet in front of their body.

If there is resistance during any of the finishes, the attacker can regain some advantage by *turning the corner*, a term you will hear other coaches use a lot. Turning the corner exaggerates the attack angle and takes away the defender's power. Keeping the head up and as tight to the body as possible and the hips

Figure 8.18 Turning the corner.

in, your wrestler steps up with the outside leg (see figure 8.18*a*) and uses a simple technique called the swisher to turn the body. To use a swisher, rotate the foot of the leg that is in the middle and still on the knee 90 degrees toward the outside foot (see figure 8.18*b*). Many times, wrestlers will suddenly find themselves looking across the back of the defender's hips. They should step up even more, pulling the far knee or hip in while exploding through the defender's body and lifting the near leg to complete the double leg (see figure 8.18*c*).

High Crotch

A high-crotch takedown is a fluid combination of an upper-body motion with a lower-level attack. Although some wrestlers may prefer keeping their distance and using minimal contact before beginning a single- or double-leg attack, a high crotch is especially effective when the opponent initiates upper-body contact. A high-crotch takedown can start from several positions, some of which are especially effective if the defender is tied up on your wrestler's head.

Starting as though using an elbow shuck, your wrestler drives the elbow in, but only enough that the defender tries to push it back (see figure 8.19a). When the attacker feels the resistance, he or she pulls the elbow back toward his or her own body and whips it behind his or her own head while changing levels and penetrating with an inside step (see figure 8.19b). The free hand goes to the back of the opponent's knee. At this point, the attacker should be on the inside knee with the outside knee up, the head on the outside of the defender's leg, and the free hand wrapping it (see figure 8.19c).

To finish the high crotch, the attacker should cut across by lifting the near leg to the side while chopping at the far knee with the arm that had been on

Figure 8.19   High-crotch takedown.

Figure 8.20 Finishing the high crotch.

Figure 8.21 Finishing the high crotch when the defender sprawls.

the inside of the opponent's legs (see figure 8.20a). Keeping the head tight to the side of the defender's body, the attacker drives up and into the defender with the outside leg, rising off the knee (see figure 8.20b). The attacker explodes into the defender at an angle while continuing to lift the leg and chopping at the far knee.

However, if the defender is able to get the hips in a sprawl, the attacker loses leverage and gets extended under his weight, making it difficult to finish the attack and also making the attacker more susceptible to counterattacks. Your wrestler can counter this by keeping the head very tight to the body, locking the arms around the leg, and keeping the body up by driving into the defender with the outside leg (see figure 8.21a). Your wrestler will start to rotate behind the defender, and when he or she has rotated enough that the head is looking across the defender's low back, your wrestler can release the lock with the arms (see figure 8.21b). Next, your wrestler can reach across with the inside hand to the far knee and rise up a bit to drive across, taking the opponent to the mat (see figure 8.21c).

Low-Level Attacks

The most common low-level attacks in youth folkstyle wrestling are the low single leg and the ankle pick.

Low Single Leg

A low-level single is a variation of the traditional single-leg takedown. Instead of attacking at the opponent's knee, the wrestler changes level even more and attacks lower on the opponent's leg. This tactic is used against an opponent with a great defense against a traditional single leg. Continuing the pitching analogy, a pitcher may use a regular fastball as well as a variation called a split-finger fastball, which is thrown straight like a regular fastball but sinks in the strike zone. The same principle is involved here. The wrestler uses a different angle of attack to provide different opportunities.

The low single is different from the other types of attacks discussed previously because it is typically started from an open position rather than from a tie-up. In a low single, the attacker uses a greater drop when changing levels, getting as low to the ground as possible while keeping the feet under the body, and then quickly attacking the lower part of the opponent's leg. Success is dictated by the dramatic change in position and the quickness of the attacker rather than by the upper-body contact that creates motion or knocks the opponent off balance.

When using the low single, your wrestlers should move in a way that causes the opponents to make the step your wrestlers want them to make. When this is done correctly and the opponent makes the step, your wrestlers should go as low as possible. In figure 8.22, the penetration step is with the outside leg. As your wrestler drives forward onto the outside knee, if the timing is right he or she will arrive at the opponent's leg just as the opponent's weight comes

Figure 8.22   Low single.

onto it, planting it (see figure 8.22*a*). With the head inside the defender's knee, the attacker cups the outside of the defender's heel with the outside hand and arm (see figure 8.22*b*). The hand of the inside arm should be just between the defender's feet, making a firm post with the upper arm to keep your wrestler from getting flattened.

There are two primary finishes to low singles.

- *Basic finish.* The basic finish is effective but needs to be done quickly. Starting with the heel cupped firmly and with the head and neck on the inside of the defender's lower knee, the offensive wrestler starts to drive the defender's trapped leg to the outside with the head (see figure 8.23*a*). At the same time, the arm that has been the post comes up to the defender's far hip and forcefully drives through the hips (see figure 8.23*b*). The offensive wrestler can roll onto the hip; keep driving with the head, neck, and free arm; and then come back up to the knees as the defender is knocked over to the side to finish (see figure 8.23*c*).

- *Out the back door.* If a defender is able to lay the body over the top of the attacker and grab an ankle or lock around the body in some way, your

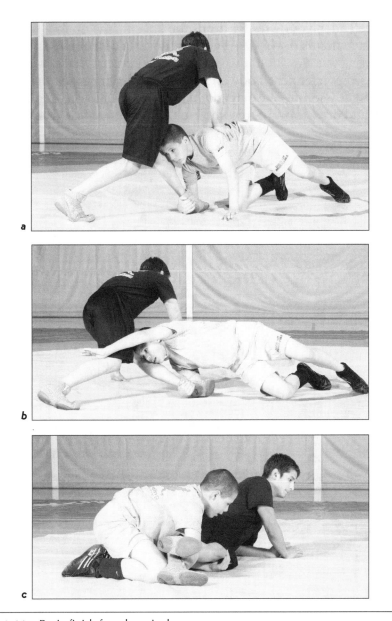

Figure 8.23   Basic finish for a low single.

wrestlers will need to know a second way to finish the low single—how to go out the back door. As quickly as possible, your wrestler should hold the cupped ankle tightly and drive the head and body up and hips forward while using the post arm to help (see figure 8.24*a*). Again, as quickly as possible, your wrestler should step up with the leg on the same side as the captured leg while driving the free arm up between the defender's legs (see figure 8.24*b*). Simultaneously, your wrestler should use an aggressive swisher with the lower leg, which is still on the mat, turning it 180 degrees (see figure 8.24*c*). When the body rotates toward the defender, your wrestler drops the knee that is up to a spot next to the knee that is down (see figure 8.24*d*). Keeping the leg trapped, the offensive wrestler should work hard to swing the free arm all the way across the defender's body and attack the far knee (see figure 8.24*e*). This tightly secures the defender's hips, and the attacker can release the heel and drive forward to complete the low single (see figure 8.24*f*).

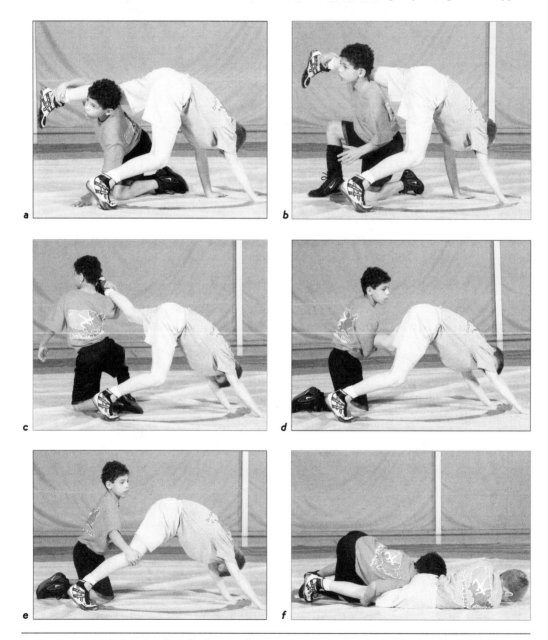

Figure 8.24 Back door finish to the low single.

Ankle Pick

During an ankle pick, which is a common takedown technique, the attacking wrestler typically uses a tie-up with one hand to try to get the opponent to step toward him or her (see figure 8.25a). Timing is key, and as the step is coming forward, the hand not used for the tie-up drops down to meet the stepping foot to cup the hand behind the heel (see figure 8.25b).

To finish the attack, the wrestler can choose to either lift the leg off the ground from that grip (see figure 8.26a) or drive the opponent straight back and off of his or her feet (see figure 8.26b).

Figure 8.25   Ankle pick.

Figure 8.26   Finish for the ankle pick.

Counterattacks

In a counterattack, wrestlers use whatever the opponent tries to do to them to their own advantage. This may mean using the momentum the opponent has created during an attack on your wrestler to knock the attacker off balance. Or your wrestler might initiate an attack while the opponent is backing out of a failed attack, which is sometimes when an opponent is the weakest defensively.

You will see many counterattacking techniques as you coach youth wrestling. However, when you begin working on counterattacks, first teach several core concepts. Your wrestlers will gain more from working on these core concepts than from working on individual techniques:

- An attacker cannot go anywhere that his or her head cannot; therefore, your wrestler's strong head position makes opponents uncomfortable in theirs and can block many techniques.

- Opponents are less apt to initiate an attack against disciplined arm position, and if they do, few attacks are successful against disciplined arm position. Your wrestlers' arms should be down with the elbows inside the body and the hands down. Your wrestlers should learn how to achieve a good inside tie-up, including one high arm (such as on the head) and one low arm (such as on a wrist or elbow) for more flexibility in moving opponents and setting up attacks.

- Wrestlers should initiate a tie-up only if they know why they are doing so and there is no obvious way for the opponent to make an offensive move through the arms. This forces opponents to do things they do not want to. Wrestlers shouldn't create contact unless they are attacking because their arms are one of the primary lines of defense against attacks on them. By holding their arms in front of them, your wrestlers create an obstacle the opponent must face while trying to reach the legs. Conversely, if your wrestlers create contact with the opponent, their arms typically move up toward the opponent's shoulders and therefore away from blocking the opponent's leg attacks.

- Stance and motion are most important. In a loose, relaxed stance, such motion makes it difficult for the attacker to get much reaction from his or her setup attempts. It also makes it possible for your wrestlers to change levels and thrust the legs and hips back quickly and powerfully when the opponent attempts a shot. In addition to maintaining motion, wrestlers should learn to anticipate moves that their opponent will make. A wrestler who can sense an oncoming attack is prepared to counter.

- Wrestlers should learn how to sprawl, which is discussed more thoroughly in the following section. Sprawls involve lowering the body while thrusting the hips and legs back as quickly as possible when an attack is launched. The goal is for the defender to end up with his or her chest on the attacker's back. A powerful sprawl and mastery of several simple techniques from the sprawl can make your wrestlers very difficult to take down.

Sprawls

If your wrestlers have quick enough reflexes, they can move side to side and out of the way of an opponent's attack toward the leg. Barring the reflexes and quickness necessary to avoid all attacks from an opponent, the first step in countering an attack is to sprawl. Consider the sprawl the starting point of defense. It stops the opponent and allows the opportunity to initiate counterattacks or defensive techniques. A sprawl in itself does not end the offense of an opponent, just like catching a ball in baseball does not necessarily end the play. Baserunners can still score unless the catcher makes the correct decisions after catching the ball and stopping the initial offensive attack. Think of the sprawl as catching the ball, and initiating the next technique as throwing the ball to the correct base to stop the runner or end the inning by getting additional outs.

When teaching sprawling, first coach your wrestlers to look at the opponent's center of gravity rather than the eyes, the feet, or anything else. Just like attackers cannot go anywhere their head cannot, they also cannot go anywhere unless they change levels. Opponents will make all sorts of feints and motions to try to get your young wrestlers to believe an attack is coming, but no matter what else is going on, the hips, as the center of gravity, control the action. Therefore, teach your wrestlers to get ready when they see the hips drop for the change in level that will become a shot.

As the shot comes, the defender must drop his or her own hips, try to block the attacker's body with the hands and arms, and thrust the legs and feet back as hard as possible (see figure 8.27). In the sprawl position—chest on the opponent's back—your wrestlers should keep their feet spread and knees off the mat so the attacker has to carry all of the weight.

Figure 8.27   Positioning for a sprawl.

When opponents shoot and your wrestlers find themselves in a sprawl situation, they should find the attacker's head instantly and push it to the mat while also blocking the side so the attacker cannot turn the corner (see figure 8.28a). They should do this every time an opponent shoots. In this situation, young wrestlers especially, but even the best wrestlers, tend to think only about their head and neck getting stuffed into the mat. That is good for your sprawling wrestlers. Depending on the situation, your wrestlers can block by using the free arm to drive into the opponent's ribs or lower abdomen. If the attacker is at an angle and has grasped a leg, your wrestler can block well

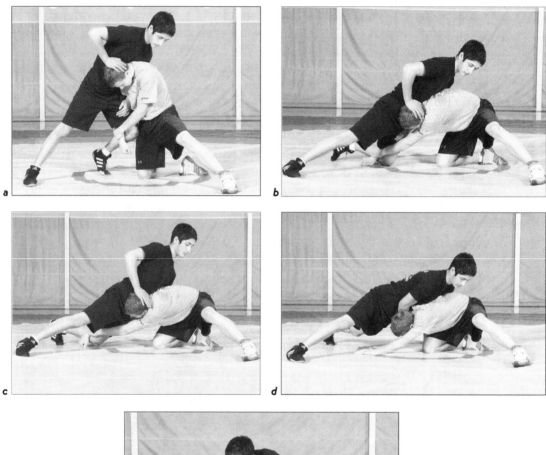

Figure 8.28   Counterattacking using a sprawl and whizzer.

with a whizzer (see figure 8.28*b*). The whizzer has your wrestler locking up the attacker's arm with the free arm and working it to control the attacker's body, while also thrusting the hips and legs down and back and pushing the head down (see figure 8.28*c*). Once the leg is free, your wrestler can release the head and grasp the near tricep of the defender (see figure 8.28*d*). Your wrestler then drops the hips even more while pulling down on the tricep so that he or she can run around the side that had been whizzered and complete the countertakedown (see figure 8.28*e*).

If the opponent does not grasp the leg, your wrestler can push the head and near arm down while sprawling (see figure 8.29*a*). When the opponent's attack has been stopped, your wrestler should release the head and use that hand and arm to reach across and block the near arm from coming up to stop the rotation while he or she goes behind on that side to score (see figure 8.29*b*). This is a simple, effective technique. To teach why this is effective, have one wrestler get on all fours on the mat. One partner should be on the knees in front of the other. The person learning will reach across to the outside of the down wrestler's far arm, with the palm facing away, and put the wrist on the upper arm near the elbow. Now, the down wrestler should try to raise the arm up and to the side, as if trying to stop the other wrestler from rotating around for the score after a sprawl. With minimal resistance, the wrestler performing the block can keep the arm down.

Figure 8.29 Counterattack by blocking the opponent's arm when he does not control the leg.

9

Coaching Top and Bottom Techniques

No matter how the wrestlers get to the mat—whether from a takedown as discussed later in this chapter or by their choice at the start of a period as discussed on page 26 of chapter 3—once there, a new kind of action begins. The top wrestler will attempt to turn the defender to the mat and secure a win by fall. Riding (the term used to describe the top wrestler's actions) well and keeping the defender down while exerting pressure are the start of working toward a fall. The bottom wrestler will attempt to get away, which is an escape, or reverse the positions and assume control from the top, which is a reversal.

Each of these positions has two basic aspects:

Top Position

1. The top wrestler must first gain or establish control and keep it—the ride.

2. Once the top wrestler has gained control, work toward the fall must begin. Constantly working toward the fall should be a special point for emphasis as you coach young wrestlers. When wrestlers have mastered several basic techniques, continuous work toward the fall results in a very aggressive ride that causes the opponent to expend a great deal of energy. Fundamentally, the top wrestler must always work to keep the bottom wrestler's hips on the mat. A wrestler cannot go anywhere his or her hips cannot.

Bottom Position

1. The bottom wrestler must first be sure to avoid exposing the back and giving up near fall points or an actual fall.

2. The bottom wrestler must then work to escape or reverse the control.

Wrestling from the top and bottom positions is an important part of a match. Although winning by fall is the ideal, technical falls (a win by 15 or more points) or major decisions (a win by 8 or more points) are next best. Such victories score more team points in dual meets (four points for a major, five for a technical fall, and six for a fall) and also get bonus points for the team in individual tournaments with team scoring. The technical fall has an additional advantage in that wrestling is stopped when there is an advantage of 15 or more points.

As shown in table 3.2 on page 28, near fall points are scored when your wrestler turns the opponent to his or her back and holds him or her there for two seconds for a two-point near fall or five seconds for a three-point near fall. Holding the shoulders to the mat for two seconds is a fall. Obviously then, the young wrestler who knows how to work aggressively on the mat, top or bottom after the takedown or choice, has a big advantage.

This chapter focuses on the skills that wrestlers need to perform effectively in youth folkstyle wrestling. Remember to use the IDEA approach to teaching skills: introduce, demonstrate, and explain the skill, and attend to wrestlers as they practice the skill (see pages 58 through 61 in chapter 6). This chapter also ties directly into the season and practice plans in chapter 11, describing the skills you'll teach during the practices outlined there. If you aren't familiar with wrestling, you may find it helpful to watch local college or high school wrestling matches or watch recordings of matches so you can see the skills performed correctly. Also, the Coaching Youth Wrestling online course offered by the American Sport Education Program (ASEP) can help you further understand these skills (you can find information about this course by going to www. ASEP.com). Additionally, because the information in this book is limited to wrestling basics, you will need to advance your coaching knowledge as your wrestlers advance in their skill development. You can do this by learning from your experiences, watching and talking with more experienced coaches, taking coaching education courses, and studying resources on advanced skills.

Starting Positions

When there is a new start situation, whether at the start of a period or after a stop in the action for some reason with one wrestler in control, the bottom wrestler assumes his or her start position—the base position—first (see figure 9.1). The hands and knees must be on the mat, outside of the starting lines. The bottom wrestler's base position is important because it also comes into play once wrestling on the mat is underway. You will hear experienced coaches encouraging their wrestlers to "Get to your base," or maybe, "Don't give up your base." Just as the top wrestler works to keep the bottom wrestler's hips down, the defender works to keep the hips off the mat. If the hips are stuck on the mat, so is the rest of the body. The higher off the mat the hips are, the better the chance of escaping or getting a reversal.

Once the bottom wrestler has assumed the base position, the official will direct the top wrestler to assume the top starting position. The top wrestler can choose one of two positions: the controlled ride or the optional start.

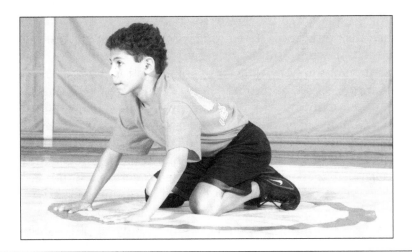

Figure 9.1   Base position for bottom wrestler.

Controlled Ride

The controlled-ride starting position is most commonly used simply because it places the top wrestler in a dominant position. With such control, the top wrestler can work for a fall or near fall, and the bottom wrestler's chances of scoring decrease.

Coaching Tip

If your wrestler is more comfortable starting the controlled-ride position from the left side, simply reverse the position in figure 9.3. Some wrestlers are more comfortable on one side or the other, and there is no particular reason to emphasize one or the other. When your wrestlers are more advanced, you and they might decide to start on a particular side in response to the strengths of an opponent.

In the controlled-ride starting position, as shown in figure 9.2, the top wrestler approaches the bottom wrestler—or defender—from either side. If approaching from the right, the top wrestler places the right knee on the mat, roughly at the defender's right knee, and places the left foot behind the defender, with the knee off the mat (see figure 9.3a). The top wrestler places the chest on the defender's back, with the left arm wrapped around the body and the palm of the left hand right on the navel of the defender (see figure 9.3b). The palm of the top wrestler's right hand is placed on the defender's right elbow, and the fingers wrap the elbow (see figure 9.3c). The top wrestler's head should face the official, with the chin at the centerline of the defender's back (see figure 9.3d).

Optional Start

The optional start is another starting position for the top wrestler. This looks more like the top starting position that has historically been used in freestyle or Greco-Roman. The top wrestler stands, and the bottom wrestler is in the base position. It is used most often when the top wrestler intends to release, or *cut*, the defender so that the defender can wrestle on the feet again. Sometimes you will hear experienced coaches encourage their wrestler to "Cut him (or her)" when they want the wrestler to release the opponent. You might hear this at the start or while action is underway on the mat.

Several situations might dictate the use of the optional start and subsequent release of the opponent from control. Most often this is because the top wrestler is better at takedowns than at turning the opponent for near fall points or a pin. This situation—releasing the defender, then scoring a takedown—results in one point to the bottom wrestler for the escape and two points to the top wrestler for the takedown for only a one-point gain. However, many falls and near falls happen as takedowns are completed. Interestingly, it is against the rules of freestyle or Greco-Roman to release the bottom wrestler.

In the optional start position, as shown in figure 9.4, the top wrestler approaches the bottom from the rear or side. Young wrestlers should place their feet similar to their position in the base position, one behind and one on the side (see figure 9.5a). The hands must be placed on the defender's

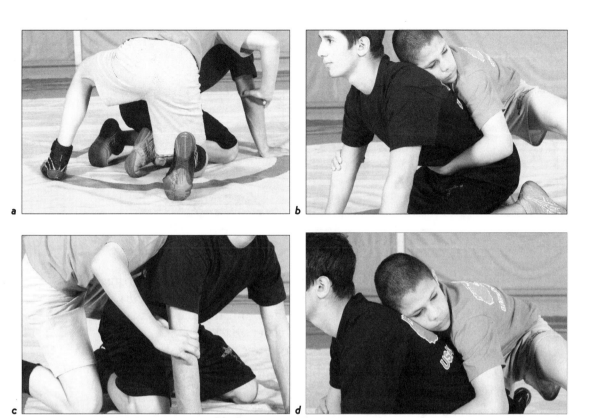

Figure 9.3 Controlled ride: *(a)* feet position, *(b)* left hand and arm position, *(c)* right hand and arm position, and *(d)* the head position.

Figure 9.4 Optional starting position for the top wrestler.

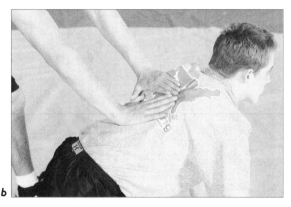

Figure 9.5 Optional start: *(a)* feet position and *(b)* hand position.

Coaching Tip

Remind young wrestlers that they must signal their intention to use the optional start to the officials so that they can alert the bottom wrestler to this. Otherwise, it is assumed that the top wrestler will use the traditional controlled-ride starting position. The bottom wrestler must be set when the top wrestler takes his or her position, and the bottom wrestler's strategy will change when it's known that the optional start will be used. If there is no advance declaration of intent, the bottom wrestler may not have a fair chance to compete in this situation. In addition, the official may want to know so that he or she can choose a better position for observing the start.

shoulder blades with the index fingers and thumbs touching (see figure 9.5*b*). The top wrestler's chest and head are away, not on the bottom wrestler's back.

When coaching young wrestlers, remind them that anything can happen with the optional start. The top wrestler can choose to explode into the bottom wrestler and take control with a ride, or the top wrestler can simply push the bottom wrestler away aggressively for an escape and not give the bottom wrestler a chance to spin quickly for his or her own score.

Top Techniques

The goal of every wrestler in the top position is to gain and maintain control of the bottom wrestler and to turn the wrestler to his or her back to achieve a pin. The ability to maintain control is vital because there are cases in which preventing an escape may win the match. Likewise, controlling the bottom wrestler is essential for turning the wrestler. Therefore, it's important that your wrestlers can effectively execute a variety of breakdowns that will put the bottom wrestler in a vulnerable position and enable them to work toward a pin.

During a match you might hear experienced coaches encourage their wrestlers to "Break him or her down" or "Get a breakdown." A breakdown can happen from the starting position or while action is underway. This means getting bottom wrestlers out of their strong, compact base position—hips up, center of gravity back, and arms and hands in a strong position. Any time bottom wrestlers are in a strong base position they can execute one of several techniques to get an escape or reversal, so it is important for top wrestlers to keep their opponent's hips on the mat.

Several conceptual elements are common to the basic breakdown and riding techniques. Coach top wrestlers to do the following:

- Keep their arms behind the bottom wrestler's shoulders to the greatest extent possible
- Keep their weight on the bottom wrestler at all times
- Constantly drive the bottom wrestler forward with their legs, hips, and chest so that the combined weight of the wrestlers is borne on the bottom wrestler's arms and hands
- Control two points on the bottom wrestler's body at all times
- Be tough and tenacious on top

Wrestlers who work on these concepts and integrate them into their top wrestling will increase their effective strength dramatically. Although these are the most basic concepts of wrestling from the top position, outstanding college wrestlers, even Olympians, need the same coaching and encouragement at all times. If these fundamentals become automatic and wrestlers develop the discipline to stick with them, they will be successful riders and will score many falls and near falls. If young wrestlers give up on one or more of these concepts during a ride, they will have trouble maintaining control, let alone securing a fall.

Four basic breakdowns that are most commonly used at the youth level are the arm chop, the spiral ride, the outside ankle breakdown, and the inside ankle breakdown (each of the breakdowns that follow are described from the controlled-ride starting position, as discussed on page 114, which is the most common starting position for a top wrestler). Each requires the top wrestler to secure two points on the opponent's body. If top wrestlers control only one, they reduce their ability to maintain control.

Arm Chop

The arm chop is the most common breakdown that coaches teach beginning wrestlers because the wrestlers do not need to move far to initiate the action. Because there are fewer steps in this technique than in others, it is easier for young wrestlers to perform it correctly. Yet when done correctly, it is effective.

To start the arm chop, the top wrestler must do several things simultaneously:

- Release the hand on the bottom wrestler's elbow so that the arm is free to chop at the inside of the elbow with the wrist or forearm (see figure 9.6).
- Use the arm that is around the bottom wrestler's waist to squeeze the abdomen as hard as possible—called a *tight waist*. This is uncomfortable,

Figure 9.6   Releasing the elbow to perform the chop.

and it helps secure the bottom wrestler's hips to the top wrestler's, eliminating the possibility of space developing (see figure 9.7a). Alternatively, the wrestler can move the hand that is on the navel to the inside of the bottom wrestler's thigh—called a *crotch pry*—locking the arm as straight as possible (see 9.7b). This also locks the opponent's hips and can be used to pry the defender over onto the hip closest to the top wrestler.

- Rise up off the knee that is on the mat, putting the legs in the loaded position, much like during the level change from the feet; keep the hips behind the opponent's; and drive forward explosively (see figure 9.8).

a

b

Figure 9.7   Arm chop: *(a)* tight waist or *(b)* crotch pry.

Figure 9.8   Rising up and loading the legs to drive forward.

The chop with forward pressure eliminates an important part of the bottom wrestler's base. It uses the combined weight of both wrestlers to eliminate the bottom wrestler's support. The bottom wrestler often goes to the mat on his or her chest or at least to an elbow. By continuing to apply pressure, the top wrestler can break down the hips all the way to the mat.

When coaching youth wrestlers, constantly remind them to continue driving even after the breakdown. Wrestlers tend to relax once the breakdown has been accomplished, which reduces the hip pressure on the opponent. If the pressure comes off, a well-coached bottom wrestler immediately comes back to the base position to initiate an escape or reversal technique. It is difficult for wrestlers to realize that their continued aggressive ride takes far more energy and confidence out of the opponent than they give up themselves. Encourage your wrestlers to watch the best teams in your area and note that the successful wrestlers who continue aggressive action while on top are much fresher than the opponent when there is a break in the action.

Spiral Ride

The spiral ride is effective, and the bottom wrestler exerts a lot of energy defending it. It uses the basic concepts outlined earlier but adds the use of torque to increase the top wrestler's power, just as it does in the back step.

To start the spiral ride from the controlled-ride starting position, again, the top wrestler does several things at once:

- The hand on the abdomen goes immediately into the crotch pry position—the palm of the hand goes to the inside of the bottom wrestler's thigh, with the arm locked in a fully straightened position (see figure 9.9).
- The hand on the bottom wrestler's elbow releases, and the top wrestler reaches through the bottom wrestler's armpit to grab the shoulder and hold it tight to his or her own chest (see figure 9.10).

- The top wrestler rises up off the knee and drives forward with the hips while levering up on the bottom wrestler's leg with the crotch pry (see figure 9.11).
- When the weight has been transferred to the bottom wrestler's arms, the top wrestler begins the spiral motion by starting to move in a circle, with the bottom wrestler's secured shoulder at the center (see figure 9.12). If starting on the right side, the spiral is counterclockwise. If starting on the left, the spiral motion is clockwise.

Figure 9.9   Spiral ride: Releasing the abdomen to gain the crotch pry position.

Figure 9.10   Spiral ride: Reaching through the armpit to secure the shoulder.

Figure 9.11   Spiral ride: Rising off the knee to drive forward.

Figure 9.12   Spiral ride: Spiraling around the axis of the opponent's shoulder.

The trick to teaching the spiral ride to youth wrestlers is to communicate the idea of driving into *and* around the opponent. The pressure must be forward even as the spiral starts the torque. Your wrestlers also need to learn to keep their hips square to the mat, and as the spiral goes farther around, they can increase their effectiveness by driving the hips into the bottom wrestler more aggressively. The spiral ride is all about leg and hip power; once again, the role of the arms is to secure the body to the offensive wrestler so that the core muscles can do the work.

As the spiral motion continues, youth wrestlers must be reminded to keep the crotch pry locked. As the spiral moves around, with a tough crotch pry the top wrestler can often move the hand securing the shoulder up into a half nelson position (see figure 9.13). To do this, the top wrestler keeps the hip, leg, and crotch pry pressure on while releasing the shoulder and reaching through a little farther, placing the hand on the back of the bottom wrestler's neck. Better yet, placing the hand at the back of the opponent's head results in more leverage.

A tough spiral ride can result in several outcomes. The opponent may end up on the hip closest to the offensive wrestler, who will then start on pinning techniques. If the top wrestler can get into the half nelson position while maintaining the pressure, the spiral may take the defender onto the outside shoulder, and then the offensive wrestler can release the crotch pry and turn the defender to the near fall position with the half nelson. If the spiral ride is aggressive and tenacious, the defender will become very tired and open up to other pin techniques later in the match.

Outside Ankle Breakdown

The outside ankle breakdown is another effective top technique. The top wrestler gets firm control of the defender's hips and uses the leverage gained from lifting the outside ankle to drive the bottom wrestler to the mat.

Figure 9.13   Spiral ride into a half nelson.

Again, the top wrestler must be able to do several things at once:

- Release the hand on the elbow so it can reach directly under the bottom wrestler's abdomen at the waist and grab the far side, resulting in a near-side tight waist (see figure 9.14).
- Release the hand on the navel and move it immediately to grasp the bottom wrestler's outside ankle at the shoelaces (see figure 9.15).
- Rise off the back knee and, using the loaded leg muscles, drive the bottom wrestler forward explosively with the legs, hips, and chest (see figure 9.16).
- Keep the bottom wrestler's ankle lifted as high as possible to keep the knee at a minimum angle, making the leg much less powerful.

Remind your wrestlers to continue this action tenaciously. They may drive the opponent all the way across the mat sometimes before achieving the breakdown, but they should keep at it, even if they have to do it over and over. It takes a tremendous amount of energy for the bottom wrestler to defend this technique, and tenacity will pay off. When wrestlers achieve the breakdown, they need to continue the forward pressure with their weight on the bottom wrestler so that he or she cannot get back to the base. If the top wrestler loses control of the ankle while driving, he or she can move into a spiral ride and continue the pressure.

Inside Ankle Breakdown

The inside ankle breakdown is another effective top technique. The position taken by the bottom wrestler sets up different breakdowns for the top wrestler. If your wrestler has been going for the outside ankle consistently, the bottom wrestler may start tucking that foot under himself or herself to prevent it.

Figure 9.14 Outside ankle breakdown: Releasing the elbow and securing a near-side tight waist.

Figure 9.15 Outside ankle breakdown: Grasping the opponent's outside ankle.

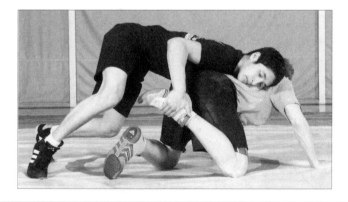

Figure 9.16 Outside ankle breakdown: Rising up to drive the opponent forward.

When that happens, the inside ankle often opens up. Your wrestlers need to recognize these subtle opportunities and adjust.

Again, the effectiveness of the inside ankle breakdown depends on the top wrestler learning to do several things at once:

- Move the hand on the bottom wrestler's elbow quickly to the near ankle, grasping it at the shoelaces (see figure 9.17).
- While controlling the ankle and maintaining the tight waist, drive the bottom wrestler forward with the legs, hips, and chest and rotate to the opposite side (see figure 9.18).
- Lift the bottom wrestler's ankle as high as possible while driving.
- Continue driving while lifting the ankle until the breakdown is complete (see figure 9.19) or the action goes out of bounds.

Encourage young wrestlers to stay off their knees and continue driving. This pressure is difficult for the bottom wrestler to resist and takes more energy to defend than it does to initiate.

Figure 9.17   Inside ankle breakdown: Releasing the elbow to grasp the opponent's near ankle.

Figure 9.18   Inside ankle breakdown: Driving the opponent forward.

Figure 9.19   Inside ankle breakdown: Driving until the breakdown is complete.

Pins

If a wrestler can *pin* both opponent's shoulders to the mat for a count of two, a *fall* is called, and the match is terminated. Little is more exciting for wrestlers than to hear the official slap the mat to indicate that they have won by fall. Of course, being on the other end is equally disappointing.

Most pins are achieved by combining techniques—called *pinning combinations*. As a new coach of youth wrestlers, you need to know the individual techniques that come together to create pinning combinations. They include the following.

Bar Arm

From the top position, ideally, with the opponent broken down, the top wrestler reaches under the bottom wrestler's near arm to grasp the wrist and pulls it back toward the bottom wrestler's waist. The top wrestler's shoulder should be on the near shoulder of the bottom wrestler, and all of the weight should be concentrated there (see figure 9.20).

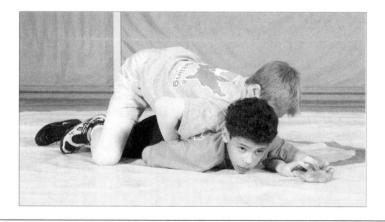

Figure 9.20   Bar arm.

Double Bar Arm

The double bar arm is thought of more as a riding technique because it refers to the two hands of the top wrestler locked on one bar arm, rather than two separate bar arms. To initiate a double bar arm, the top wrestler may start from the tight waist position, as shown in figure 9.21*a*, and pull down the bar arm. Then the top wrestler can release the tight waist and use that hand to join the other on the bar arm (see figure 9.21*b*). This is a tough riding position, but it is an effective way to *tilt*—turn to a near fall position without the control necessary to achieve a fall—the defender for near fall points.

Figure 9.21   Double bar arm.

Chicken Wing

The chicken wing is a lock on the bottom wrestler's arm to take it out of play. It is most often used in combination with a bar arm or half nelson. Together they make a tough ride and an even tougher pinning combination. The top wrestler reaches around and under the bottom wrestler's arm from the outside above the elbow and completes the chicken wing by pushing the arm through so that the top wrestler's forearm ends up on the bottom wrestler's back with the palm down (see figure 9.22).

Figure 9.22   Chicken wing.

Double Chicken Wing

The double chicken wing is just what it says, a chicken wing on both sides. To make the double chicken wing tighter, the top wrestler reaches through far enough to lock the hands together (see figure 9.23*a*), or even farther so that the hands can grasp each of the defender's arms above the elbows (see figure 9.23*b*).

Hammerlock

The hammerlock is a powerful riding technique used for tilting or in pinning combinations, as discussed later on pages 131 through 139. To use a hammerlock, the top wrestler starts with a bar arm, then pulls the bottom wrestler's arm outside the body enough that it can be placed on the bottom wrestler's own back (see figure 9.24).

Crossface

The crossface can be used in a variety of situations, and it is an effective component of several pinning combinations, as discussed later on pages 131 through 139. For the crossface, from the top position on the right side, the top wrestler's right arm reaches across the front of the bottom wrestler's face to grasp the bottom wrestler's upper arm (see figure 9.25). The top wrestler

Figure 9.23   Variations for the double chicken wing.

Figure 9.24   Hammerlock.

Figure 9.25   Crossface.

can use his or her radius (the bone on the thumb side of the forearm) to create discomfort for the bottom wrestler when the bony forearm comes in contact with the bottom wrestler's facial bones, temple, or forehead.

Half Nelson

Half nelson is a wrestling term that most people, even those not familiar with wrestling, have heard before. It is half of a full nelson, which is illegal in folkstyle wrestling. It is most commonly used to turn the bottom wrestler from his or her base to the back and into a near fall or pin situation. The top wrestler reaches through the bottom wrestler's armpit from behind deeply enough that the top wrestler can bring that hand up and place it across the bottom wrestler's neck or, ideally, at the back of the bottom wrestler's head (see figure 9.26a). This phase of the half nelson can be used as a ride to maintain control over the bottom wrestler, as in the spiral ride or as a half nelson and bar arm ride, or it can be used as a lever to turn the bottom wrestler to a near fall position. Once in the near fall position, the top wrestler must maintain a chest-to-chest position with the bottom wrestler and drive the half nelson arm back under the bottom wrestler's neck so that it circles the neck as completely as possible (see figure 9.26b).

a

b

Figure 9.26 Half nelson.

Reverse Half Nelson

The reverse half nelson is used when the bottom wrestler is on his or her back, and the top wrestler's chest is on the bottom wrestler's chest. The reverse half is used when it is difficult to subdue the bottom wrestler any other way. If the bottom wrestler rocks wildly from side to side while your wrestler is applying a half nelson, the half nelson may loosen up. In that case, it may be necessary to *reverse the half* and try to gain control of the hips with the other hand by placing it on the mat between the opponent's legs. For the reverse half nelson, the top wrestler should first be at a 90-degree angle to the bottom wrestler's body (see figure 9.27a). The top wrestler's arm that is closest to the bottom wrestler's head is then placed under the bottom wrestler's neck (see figure 9.27b) to prevent him or her from rolling away and out of the near fall situation.

a

b

Figure 9.27   Reverse half nelson.

Grapevine

The grapevine is a leg hold by the top wrestler on the bottom wrestler's leg and is one component of several rides and pinning combinations. The top wrestler's leg wraps the bottom wrestler's leg from the outside (see figure 9.28a), and the lower leg and foot end up going from the inside over the

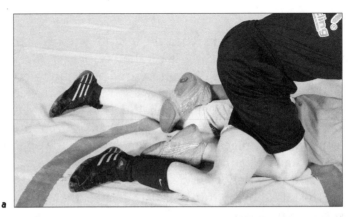

Figure 9.28   Grapevine.

back of the defender's calf (see figure 9.28*b*) and hooking on the outside of the bottom wrestler's lower leg. It is important for the top wrestler to keep his or her hips on top of the bottom wrestler's hips, with the bulk of the top wrestler's body weight across the body.

Figure Four

The top wrestler initiates a figure four by wrapping his or her legs around the defender's leg. For the figure four, first imagine a 4. The bottom wrestler's leg is through the hole in the four, while the vertical line of the 4 is one of the top wrestler's legs, and the angled line is the top wrestler's other leg, locked behind the knee of the straight leg, above the defender's knee. The figure four on the leg is used much like the grapevine, and the top wrestler must keep the hips and body positioned the same way. It can be done inside or outside the opponent's leg and can generate a great deal of pressure. A wrestler makes an inside figure four by scooping between the opponent's legs. For example, assuming your wrestler is on top, to trap the opponent's right leg with an inside figure four, your wrestler scoops his or her left (bent) leg under the opponent's right and locks it behind his or her own right (straight) leg (see figure 9.29). An outside figure four scoops from the

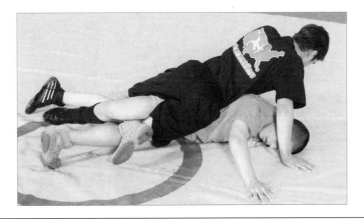

Figure 9.29   Inside figure four.

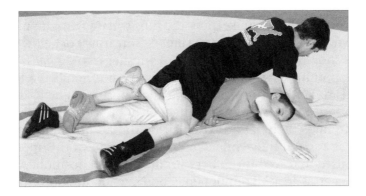

Figure 9.30   Outside figure four.

outside. For example, again assuming your wrestler is on top, to trap the opponent's right leg with an outside figure four, your wrestler scoops his or her own right (bent) leg under the opponent's right and locks it behind his or her own left (straight) leg (see figure 9.30).

It is difficult to pin a tough opponent using just one of the techniques we have discussed by itself. That's where pinning combinations come into play. For example, with just a half nelson in place, the bottom wrestler can rock back and forth to keep a shoulder off the mat and avoid the pin. However, when your wrestler uses the half nelson and a bar arm or other technique, he or she has tight control of the opponent and will be able to achieve the pin. Here are several examples of how to pair two techniques to pin an opponent:

Half Nelson and Bar Arm

When top wrestlers use a bar arm on the far side and a half nelson on the near side, bottom wrestlers have difficulty countering the leverage that forces them into a near fall position (see figure 9.31). For this combination, the top wrestler should be off the knees, driving into and around the head of

Figure 9.31   Half nelson and bar arm.

the bottom wrestler while keeping the hips square with the mat—that is, belly down, and the shoulder of the half nelson arm at or below the bottom wrestler's shoulder to force the bottom wrestler into a near fall position. Once the bottom wrestler is in a near fall position and the top wrestler can get his or her body into a chest-to-chest position at a 90-degree angle to the bottom wrestler and maintain control of both holds, this becomes a tight pinning combination. The half nelson and bar arm combination also acts as a tough ride while working to wear down the opponent until it can be used to force him or her into the near fall position. As discussed earlier, the arms lock the opponent's body, while the powerful hips and legs do most of the work.

Half Nelson and Chicken Wing

This combination is similar to the half nelson and bar arm. Bottom wrestlers cannot defend against the leverage that forces them into a near fall position when top wrestlers use a chicken wing on the far side and a half nelson on the near side (see figure 9.32). If the top wrestler can maintain both holds,

Figure 9.32   Half nelson and chicken wing.

this pinning combination is even tighter once the bottom wrestler is in a near fall position.

This combination can be so tight that the top wrestler may have to adjust and let the bottom wrestler's body move through so he or she can go to the back. Once the bottom wrestler is in the near fall position and the top wrestler can get his or her body into a chest-to-chest position at a 90-degree angle to the bottom wrestler and maintain control of both holds, this becomes a tight pinning combination. The half nelson and chicken wing combination also acts as a tough ride while working to wear down the opponent until it can be used to force him or her into the near fall position.

Chicken Wing and Bar Arm

With a chicken wing on the far side, a top wrestler can reach through with the free arm into a tight waist (see figure 9.33a). Often, the bottom wrestler will try to drive the arm in the chicken wing deeper under to resist the pressure that the chicken wing creates against the body. If the bottom wrestler's arm in the chicken wing comes through deep enough, the top wrestler can grasp the wrist with the tight waist arm (see figure 9.33b). Once the wrist is grasped (bar arm), the bottom wrestler's body is encircled, and he or

Figure 9.33   Chicken wing and bar arm.

Roll Variation for the Half Nelson and Bar Arm

As your wrestlers become more comfortable with the half nelson, bar arm, and chicken wing pinning combinations, they will start to notice that the bottom wrestlers will do whatever they can to resist going into a near fall position. Typically, the bottom wrestler will try to turn away from the top wrestler while bracing with the outside leg. If the bottom wrestler's resistance is tough, the top wrestler can learn to roll with the resistance pressure that is coming back into him or her while aggressively maintaining both holds. To do this, the top wrestler should use the half nelson arm to drive the bottom wrestler's elbow forward so that it cannot resist this new pressure (see figure 9.34a), then drive the outside knee as deep under the bottom wrestler as possible while rolling the bottom wrestler over the top (see figure 9.34b). If the top wrestler is on the right side, he or she will roll onto the right side, and then all the way under and through and come back up. If on the left, the roll goes to the left and again under the bottom wrestler. As the roll continues and the top wrestler comes back on top, he or she must get the body back into a 90-degree angle and hold the bottom wrestler in the near fall position (see figure 9.34c).

a

b

c

Figure 9.34 Roll variation being used with the half nelson and bar arm.

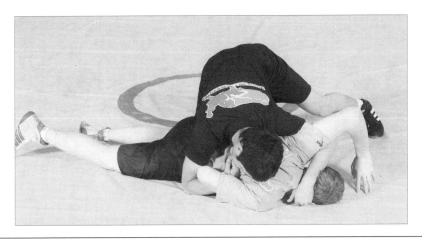

Figure 9.35 Chicken wing and bar arm into a half nelson.

she is vulnerable to being turned onto the back. At the same time, the top wrestler should be up off the knees and should use the legs and hips to drive into the bottom wrestler, creating pressure. The top wrestler can drive until there is resistance, then use the resistance pressure to roll away from the chicken wing, driving the outside knee under the bottom wrestler and rolling through until the bottom wrestler is in a near fall position—called a tilt (see figure 9.33c). The top wrestler may also find it effective to roll all the way through, and as he or she starts to come up on top again, to release the tight waist and slip that arm up into a half nelson while maintaining the chicken wing (see figure 9.35). Again, it is important get the body out to 90 degrees.

Double Chicken Wing

The double chicken wing can be turned into a pinning combination if the top wrestler keeps it locked up and rotates his or her body around the bottom wrestler's head. For this combination, the top wrestler is off the knees with the hips square to the mat and assumes a double chicken wing hold on the bottom wrestler. If the top wrestler is on the left side of the bottom wrestler, the rotation goes around the defender's head clockwise by walking the feet (if on the right, the rotation is counterclockwise). This is initiated by driving forward and toward the opponent's far side (right shoulder). As the rotation starts to go around the bottom wrestler's head, the outside (right) shoulder will be pinned tight to the mat (see figure 9.36a). To turn the opponent, the top wrestler walks the feet forward, coming around the head using the opponent's shoulder on the mat as the axis of the rotation (see figure 9.36b). As the rotation continues, the top wrestler should continue to stay square with the mat, that is, face it with the face, body, and hips. Some adjustment of the double chicken wing may be necessary to allow the defender to go over into a near fall position, and the top wrestler will learn to feel that. There is no need to rush

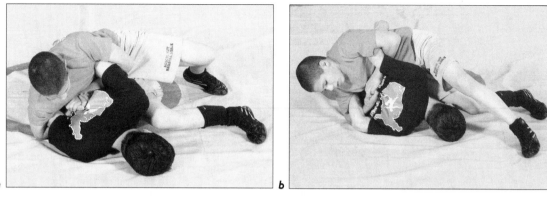

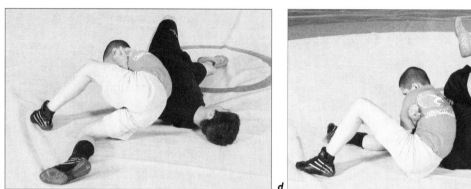

Figure 9.36   Double chicken wing as a pinning combination.

this move unless time in the period is short. The action should continue this way until the defender's shoulders are square with the mat (see figure 9.36c). To complete the fall, it may be necessary for the top wrestler to *sit out*, which means that while maintaining the double chicken wing hold, the top wrestler takes the leg closest to the opponent's head and sits it all the way through until the controlling wrestler is now face, body, and hips up (see figure 9.36d).

Hammerlock and Crossface

If the top wrestler has a near-side bar arm hold on the bottom wrestler, and the bottom wrestler is completely broken down, the top wrestler can pull the bar out and into a hammerlock (see figure 9.37a). The top wrestler can adjust the grip on the hammerlock so that both hands are grasping the wrist in a baseball grip, like you would hold a bat (see figure 9.37b). If on the left side, the top wrestler maintains the hammerlock with the right hand while using the left to get a firm crossface (see figure 9.37c). The top wrestler adjusts so that his or her chest is at the bottom wrestler's shoulder and drives the hammerlock to the bottom wrestler's outside hip while levering with the crossface and adjusting it to pull the opponent's outside arm across the chest and driving with the hips and legs (see figure 9.37d).

As the defender starts to go over into a near fall situation, the top wrestler adjusts so that the wrestlers are chest to chest with the top at 90 degrees to the bottom and in a reverse half nelson. It will be necessary for the top wrestler to also control the bottom wrestler's crotch to fully control this situation (see figure 9.37*e*).

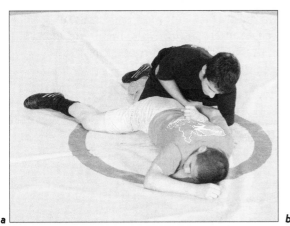
a

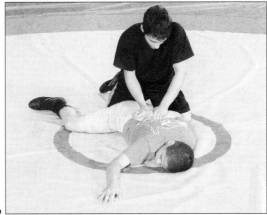
b

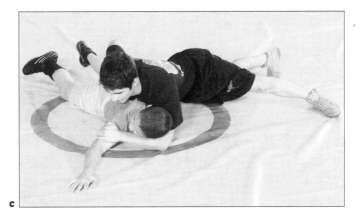
c

d

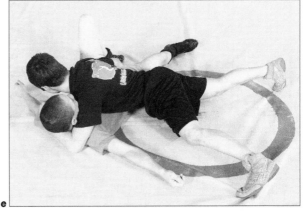
e

Figure 9.37 Hammerlock and crossface.

Leg Ride and Crossface Into a Turk

The turk position evolves from a leg ride, such as the grapevine or figure four, and is used to control the lower half of the bottom wrestler. The turk pinning combination is achieved by starting with a strong leg ride then using the arm closest to the opponent's head to grasp a strong crossface, reaching through far enough that the hand of the crossface arm can grasp the shoulder or upper arm of the defender (see figure 9.38*a*). The top wrestler arches his back and lifts his legs (which will turn the head and lift the inside hip of the bottom wrestler) to turn the bottom wrestler to the near fall position (see figure 9.38*b*). As the defender starts to go over, the

Figure 9.38   Figure four and crossface into a turk.

top wrestler can adjust the crossface so that the inside of that elbow is just under the opponent's chin, and the hand is placed on top of the opponent's head (see figure 9.38c).

Bottom Techniques

Wrestling from the bottom position can be difficult for young wrestlers because they have to be thinking about getting an escape or reversal while also fighting off the opponent's attempts to gain a pin. Often, top wrestlers are described as having the advantage, and they really do. If they are well coached, they will make the bottom wrestler carry their weight, and they will drive forward, using their leg and hip muscles.

The base position, discussed on page 113, is the bottom wrestler's starting position. If a wrestler gets broken down and the pressure continues, it becomes apparent there isn't much he or she can do while laying facedown on the mat. Indeed, you will hear other coaches encouraging their bottom wrestlers to "Get off your belly." Coaches really mean "Get back to your base." The base position is important because when the abdomen is off the mat and the hips are up, the bottom wrestler can start trying to escape or gain a reversal.

Just as there are several concepts that you can work on with your wrestlers when they are on top, there are also specific concepts that wrestlers should learn when they are the bottom wrestler:

Coaching Tip
When starting in the bottom position or just after giving up a takedown, it is important that youth wrestlers don't give up their base, or get broken down. That said, it is generally better to coach proactively than reactively or preventively. Although "Don't give up your base" is an important idea, it is negative. "Build your base" is positive. Work with your wrestlers to develop a strong base. Developing a core concept of working to get and keep the hips up allows you to emphasize the positive more often.

- *Keep the hips from going to the mat.*

  Once down, the bottom wrestler must try to get elevation. If the bottom wrestler hasn't allowed the top wrestler to drive him or her all the way down, the bottom wrestler has a sort of head start. If the bottom wrestler is all the way down, not only does he or she have a lot of work to do to simply gain elevation, but it is doubled or maybe tripled because of the opponent's weight and pressure. Coach your wrestlers to resist going all the way down, whether by a breakdown or takedown, and to think about coming back up instantly.

- *Create space.*

  The bottom wrestler must work to create space between his or her hips and the top wrestler's hips. Almost all escape and reversal techniques depend on getting separation between the bottom and top wrestlers' hips. This concept can be applied in many situations. If the defender starts working to separate the hips from the attacker's on the way down, the attacker will be in a weaker position when he or she hits the mat. That said, if the defender can get even one foot down on the way to the mat, her or she can start walking the hips away so there is already separation when they both hit the mat. In addition, skills to be learned later, such as sit-outs, switches, and hip-heists, are all designed to achieve this separation.

- *Get back to the base position.*

  Bottom wrestlers must work quickly to get the hips up back into the base position after a takedown. Statistically, most near fall or pin situations happen in conjunction with takedowns. This may be because young wrestlers often try to catch their breath or take a few seconds before they start working from the bottom once in the bottom position after a takedown. However, if the bottom wrestler continually works to get the hips up off the mat and does so as quickly as possible after a takedown, the top wrestler will be busy trying to counteract that rather than focusing on getting set for a pinning combination. This is a concept, and maybe a matter of attitude, that you can drill until it becomes instinctive for your wrestlers. If young wrestlers can grasp this early, they will find more success while in the bottom position.

- *Feel the pressure.*

  Bottom wrestlers must feel where the top wrestler's pressure comes from. Many techniques are based on meeting the top wrestler's pressure and then using it to help the bottom wrestler come up to the feet by meeting the resistance.

- *Work quickly.*

  Bottom wrestlers should work quickly so that they do not give the top wrestler chances to settle into dominating positions.

- *Know when to use torque.*

  Bottom wrestlers must learn to feel when to use torque with the hip-heist. The hip-heist, or rotating the hips 180 degrees or more while also spinning the body 180 degrees or more, is a powerful twisting movement that becomes a key part of many techniques.

- *Wrestle defensively.*

  Teach your wrestlers to think of bottom wrestling as a type of attack on the top wrestler, meaning that if young wrestlers are taught to think of it as defense, they will learn the concept of wrestling defensively. Bottom wrestlers must have a plan, so help them plan their attack from the bottom so that they know what they will do before the top wrestler assumes his or her position. The top wrestler's position can dictate the best technique for the bottom wrestler. When top wrestlers are fairly high on the bottom wrestler's back, it's likely that they will work on arm chops or spiral rides. When top wrestlers are well back, it is more likely they will try one of the ankle picks.

The young wrestler's plan when in the bottom position should include several options to cover a variety of situations. For instance, your wrestler might be thinking about an inside stand-up and going through the steps in his or her head, but if the top wrestler comes on high, your wrestler should be able to switch to a limp-arm stand-up or another technique.

These concepts come together as your wrestlers use specific bottom-wrestling techniques such as stand-ups and switches.

Stand-Up

A stand-up is a technique for achieving an escape and can be used from the starting position on the mat or during action. The name describes the technique: The wrestler must get to a standing position from the bottom and then complete the escape by turning to face the defender. Although a stand-up is a basic move, when it is done well, it is difficult to counter.

When your wrestler assumes the bottom position with a stand-up in mind, the head should be up with the arms slightly bent and very little weight on the hands (see figure 9.39a). The wrestler's weight should be as far back and as high as possible, and he or she should try to hunch, or curve, the back up

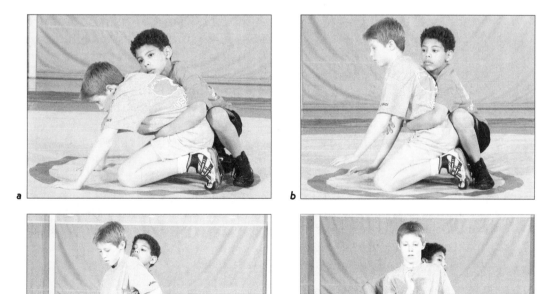

Figure 9.39 Positioning for a stand-up.

high. This elevates the weight before the action starts so there is less distance to travel to get to the feet. And keeping most of the wrestler's weight off the hands counters the effectiveness of an opponent's arm chop.

When the whistle initiates the action, the bottom wrestler explosively thrusts the arms and hands into the mat to drive the head, shoulders, and torso up and back to meet the top wrestler's forward pressure (see figure 9.39b). As the bottom wrestler starts to come up, his or her outside hand should quickly cover the top wrestler's hand that is on the waist and grasp it firmly (see figure 9.39c). As the bottom wrestler comes up, the elbow of the inside arm goes directly to the wrestler's own hip, with the wrist up, to prevent the top wrestler from shooting the hand through that has been on the elbow and locking hands as the bottom wrestler comes up (see figure 9.39d).

The bottom wrestler has several options for the inside arm and chooses one depending on how the top wrestler reacts. If the top wrestler chops, the bottom wrestler can "limp arm" by relaxing the inside arm so that as the chop comes and the bottom wrestler is coming up and grasping the hand on the abdomen, the bottom wrestler lets the limp arm go with the chop. The hand should go to about the hip, with the thumb on the inside (see figure 9.40a), and as the bottom wrestler comes up, the upper body twists a quarter turn away from the top wrestler and the hand is pulled straight up the side of the body, leading with the elbow until the hand is up near the armpit (see figure 9.40b). At this point, the arm is thrust straight up to prevent it from being grasped, while maintaining the cover on the waist hand (see figure 9.40c).

If the top wrestler jams his or her elbow forward, the bottom wrestler explodes and covers the hand as described here. But instead of bringing the elbow in, or limping the arm, the near arm can be driven up and across the bottom wrestler's chest to clear it (see figure 9.41). These techniques work because of the cover on the waist hand. If the top wrestler is able to reach through to attempt a lock around the waist, he or she will be able to grasp only the bottom wrestler's hand that is covering, and this can be dealt with.

Now that you have learned about the positioning and movements for your bottom wrestler's upper body and arms, let's discuss several types of stand-ups that require different leg positioning and movement. The following are the stand-ups most common at the youth level:

- *Inside stand-up.* Inside stand-ups are effective because they require the bottom wrestler to get the inside leg up first to resist the drive that can come with an arm chop. When top wrestlers apply forward pressure and chop the inside arm, bottom wrestlers can go to their abdomen unless they thrust upward and step the inside leg out to resist the pressure. This stand-up is done in two counts: The explosion, cover, and block described previously and the inside leg movement happen simultaneously, and then the outside leg comes up. As the head, chest, and torso come up to meet the pressure from the top wrestler, the inside leg steps to about the spot where the inside hand of the bottom wrestler had been on the

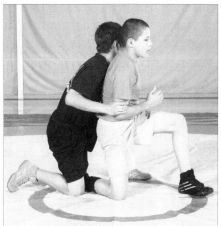

Figure 9.40   Inside-arm option for the stand-up when the top wrestler uses a chop.

Figure 9.41   Inside-arm option for the stand-up when the top wrestler jams the elbow forward.

mat (see figure 9.42*a*). Next, the outside leg comes up to form a strong, wide position (see figure 9.42*b*).

- *Outside stand-up.* Use an outside stand-up against wrestlers who use an outside ankle pick from the top position. This stand-up occurs in two counts: The explosion, cover, and block and the outside leg movement happen simultaneously, and then the inside leg comes up. Although the explosion, cover, and inside-arm techniques are the same as described earlier, the pressure from the top wrestler can be different; therefore, the bottom wrestler should feel it and pressure into it. As the head, chest, and torso come up to meet the pressure from the top wrestler, the outside leg steps to about the spot where the bottom wrestler's outside hand had been on the mat (see figure 9.43*a*). Next, the inside leg comes up to form a wide and solid position (see figure 9.43*b*).

Figure 9.42   Inside stand-up.

Figure 9.43   Outside stand-up.

- *Limp-arm stand-up.* The limp-arm option, discussed on page 142, focused on the arm movement. However, the limp-arm option uses specific leg movements, as well. For the limp-arm stand-up, the bottom wrestler explodes up into the top wrestler and begins the limp arm and quarter turn as discussed earlier. In this one-count stand-up, the bottom wrestler pivots on the toes of the outside foot, and at the same time, the inside leg comes up.

After using one of these stand-ups, the bottom wrestler should be on his or her feet with the top wrestler behind. At this point, the bottom wrestler is in control of the situation with the hand on the waist covered. To finish the stand-up, coach your wrestlers to do the following:

- Keep the knees bent so that his or her center of gravity is lower than the top wrestler's. Keep the back straight, head up, and the feet moving so that the top wrestler cannot get set (see figure 9.44*a*).
- Bring both hands to the one that is covered and remove it from the waist by extending the arms straight out (see figure 9.44*b*).
- With two hands on one, the hips low, back straight, and feet moving, increase the pressure by dropping the hips down and then out—away from the top wrestler—to increase the separation between hips. The key is to get good separation and make the turn to face the opponent with an aggressive back step (see figure 9.44*c*).

Figure 9.44 Finishing a stand-up.

Switch

Switches are moves in which the wrestlers switch positions. Switches are based on the side hip-heist, a technique that generates force similar to that of the back step on the feet. The hip-heist generates power with a quick rotation of the hips within a small amount of space. For the hip-heist, from the bottom, or base, position (see figure 9.45*a*), the wrestler starts by reaching across the body with the inside arm while turning the body outside, away from the top wrestler, and pivoting on the outside foot (see figure 9.45*b*). Sometimes the wrestler steps the outside foot up and out a bit to make room for the body to rotate. As he or she turns the body away, the wrestler should aggressively rotate the hips so that the inside leg moves outside, past the pivot (see figure 9.45*c*). Ideally, the rotation generates enough motion that the bottom wrestler lands on what was the outside hip (see figure 9.45*d*). The bottom wrestler's outside arm and elbow should be tight to the body so that as the rotation completes, it can be driven between the two wrestlers' bodies with all the force of the hip-heist and the arm.

Where the wrestler's hip lands is less important than how the wrestler lands. Completing the motion so that it is landed on what was the outside hip is the key to this forceful movement. The traditional outside switch focuses on the bottom wrestler making the rotation and landing on both buttocks while reaching with the hand closest to the defender to catch the inside of the top wrestler's near leg and then working to lever the opponent's body to the mat. Aggressively completing the hip-heist while driving the arm down can result in the bottom wrestler being in a loaded position to drive into the new defender and completing a reversal that looks very much like a takedown. It can also result in an escape, with the defender in a poor position to defend a takedown attempt. Finally, it can be finished the same as a traditional switch. If the hip-heist is completed explosively, there will be less resistance from the opponent.

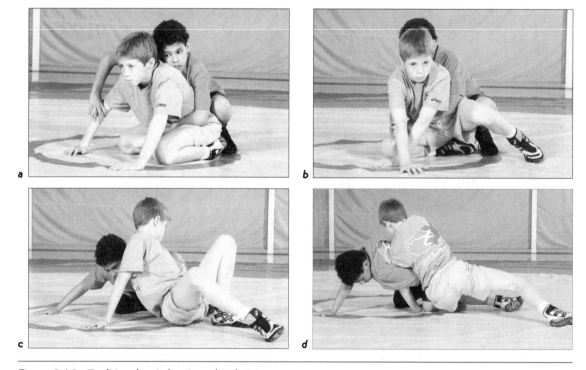

Figure 9.45 Traditional switch using a hip-heist.

The hip-heist can also be an explosive single move that generates a quick escape. In this case, the hip-heist goes less to the side, as in a switch, and more out in front. The bottom wrestler steps up and forward with the outside foot while doing the same with the inside hand (see figure 9.46a). Driving off the inside hand and outside foot, the bottom wrestler moves the inside leg out in front, roughly lined up with the top wrestler's body (see figure 9.46b). Rotating the hips, the bottom wrestler lands on the outside hip while driving the outside elbow straight down to the mat as close to the body as possible. If the top wrestler has been able to follow and keep the arm in there, this will knock it off (see figure 9.46c). The inside leg comes up and over the outside

Figure 9.46 Escaping from the bottom with an explosive hip-heist.

(see figure 9.46*d*), and the bottom wrestler turns to face the new defender while coming up to begin an attack (see figure 9.46*e*).

Further, some wrestlers may use a sit-out and turn-in move, which involves the bottom wrestler stepping up just a bit with the outside leg while sitting out in front of the starting position and landing on the inside hip. The turn-in is completed by bringing the outside leg up and over the inside and rolling the body that way, ending up facing where the top wrestler had been on hands and knees.

Of course, the top wrestler will follow the action, and it is not uncommon for him or her to escape. However, the bottom wrestler may well use a sit-out as part of a series of moves to develop space between the hips so that he or she can complete another move such as a stand-up.

Effective top and bottom techniques are the key to folkstyle wrestling. Coaches teach a variety of breakdown and pinning combinations and escapes and reversals. And then the very best wrestlers put these basic moves together while maintaining great position to develop what seems like spectacular action. And it is; however, the key is that they are executing the basics extremely well. There are more complicated techniques, but wrestlers have to be extremely skilled or powerful to make them work effectively. So there really is not much point when the basics can be as effective, and performing them well can help equalize strength and experience.

10

Coaching
Competitions

M atches provide opportunities for your wrestlers to show what they've learned in practice. Just as your wrestlers' focus shifts on competition days from learning and practicing to competing, your focus shifts from teaching skills to coaching wrestlers as they perform those skills in matches. Of course, competition is a teaching opportunity as well, but the focus is on performing what has been learned, participating, and having fun.

In previous chapters you learned how to teach your wrestlers the skills of wrestling; in this chapter you will learn how to coach your wrestlers as they execute those skills in matches. We provide important coaching principles that will guide you before, during, and after a match.

Before the Competition

Many coaches focus on how they will coach only during the actual match; instead, preparations should begin well before the first blow of the whistle. A day or two before a competition, you should cover several subjects—in addition to the skills of wrestling—to prepare your wrestlers. Depending on the age group you are working with, create a specific competition plan for the opponent based on information available to you; make decisions on specific team tactics that you want to use; and discuss precompetition particulars such as what to eat before a match, what to wear, and when to be at the gym.

Coaching Tip

Based on the age level, experience, and knowledge of your wrestlers, you may want to let them help you determine the warm-up sequence for competitions. Allowing athlete input involves them at a planning level often reserved solely for the coach and gives them a feeling of ownership. Rather than just carrying out the coach's orders, they're executing the plan that they helped create. It is important to provide guidance and make sure that the plan includes what you need it to as well as what they'd like. This is an opportunity for you to help the wrestlers understand the warm-up, how it works, and why it is important for their performance.

Deciding Team Tactics

Competition tactics at the youth level don't need to be complex—especially for the younger age groups. The main focus should be the importance of basic skills; keeping kids focused on these essential skills helps them understand the sport and be successful. If you know specific techniques that a team or teams at an upcoming competition will use, spend a bit more time on the applicable basic techniques that will prepare them to deal with those situations. The older the age group and the more familiar you become with each wrestler's tendencies and abilities, the more you can help them focus on specific tactics. For example, if your athletes have a tendency to stand up and relax or to come out of their stances at critical times during a match, you may want to emphasize the importance of staying in a sound position ready to shoot or react, especially on the edge of the mat.

Creating a Competition Plan

Just as you need a practice plan for what you will cover at each practice, you also need a plan for competitions. Your match plan for youth wrestling will vary depending on the age group you work with. As you begin planning and mapping out how your match days will progress, keep the following age-related points in mind.

Age	Tips
6-9	• Encourage wrestlers to try their best. • Focus on helping the wrestlers develop the seven basic skills. • As you teach moves, emphasize bringing the basic skills together to form techniques. • Help the wrestlers understand the concepts (why the moves work). • Emphasize practice over competition—two practices to one competition is a good rule of thumb. • Emphasize fun, sportsmanship, and teamwork.
10-12	• Focus on helping your team execute the skills they have learned. • Use simple strategies that take advantage of the concepts and skills learned in practice. • Help the wrestlers develop an offensive and defensive plan for their matches. • Encourage the wrestlers to try the techniques they learn at practice in the competitions. • Continue to emphasize fun, sportsmanship, and teamwork.
13-14	• Encourage wrestlers to be aware of the techniques and strategies other teams use regularly and to prepare for them when possible. • Remind wrestlers that although they will sometimes adjust their strategy to counter an opponent, is still most important to properly execute the techniques and skills learned in practice. • Begin to apply more advanced techniques that build on the basics. • Continue to emphasize fun, sportsmanship, and teamwork.

During the week before a competition, coaches of older age groups, such as the 12 to 14 age groups, should work with wrestlers on the tactics that they plan to use against a particular opponent. Regardless of the tactical adjustments you might make for a particular opponent, remember that it is far more important to teach wrestlers to properly execute the basic skills and focus their attention on bringing to the match the skills they have learned in practice.

Discussing Precompetition Preparations

Athletes need to know what to do before a match, such as what and when they should eat on the day of the competition, what clothing to wear to the event, what equipment to bring, what time to arrive, and how the warm-up will run. Discuss these particulars with them at the last practice before a competition. Here are guidelines for discussing these issues.

Precompetition Meal

The general goals of the prematch meal are to fuel the wrestler for the upcoming event, maximize carbohydrate stores, and provide energy to the brain. Some foods, such as those containing carbohydrate and protein, digest more quickly than others; we suggest that athletes consume these foods rather than those containing fat, which digest more slowly. Good choices for carbohydrate foods include spaghetti, rice, and bran. Good choices for protein include low-fat yogurt and boneless, skinless chicken. Wrestlers should eat foods that they are familiar with and that they can digest easily. Big meals should be eaten at least three hours before most athletic contests, and this can be a problem for wrestling. Weigh-in procedures have been changed at most levels, moving them closer to the start of competition to discourage the excessive weight loss that requires more time for recovery. The meal that provides fuel for competition may need to be eaten early in the day or the evening before. This is another reason to use more complex carbohydrate in a well-balanced meal. When the weigh-in is just an hour or so before the start of the competition, wrestlers may consume sport beverages and a light snack before their first match, then rehydrate and refuel after matches throughout the competition.

Clothing and Equipment

Make sure that the wrestlers understand your expectations for dress on the day of the competition. If your team or club has jackets, sweatshirts, or T-shirts that you would like them to wear to and from competitions and specific uniforms for competition, you should stress this at the parent-orientation meeting at the beginning of the season and at the practices immediately before each competition.

Arrival Time

Plan to arrive at the site at least half an hour before the start of the weigh-in. This allows adequate time to check in, try out the scale, go to the restroom, go through the skin-check procedure, and so on. Once the team has gone through the weigh-in, wrestlers should have a light snack and drinks as discussed earlier, then dress for the competition. Once dressed, take the group to the gymnasium so there is adequate time for a team warm-up (which you will read about in a later section).

The team warm-up is a time to stretch and work the large muscle groups. Incorporate drills that reinforce the basic skills so that their importance is fresh in the young wrestler's mind. This team activity could last 20 to 30 minutes and might also include some talk time to help focus the athletes on the things they've been practicing. Some wrestlers will not compete for quite a while following the team warm-up; others will get started sooner.

All of the wrestlers should go through a shorter second warm-up just before their match. You and the wrestlers should know the schedule so there is time for this second warm-up before competing. The appropriate amount of time depends on the age group. Following are suggested times for youth age groups.

- *Ages 6 to 8*: 10 minutes before match time
- *Ages 9 to 14*: 15 minutes before match time

Warm-Up

Athletes need to prepare both physically and mentally for a match once they are weighed in, refreshed, and dressed. Physical preparation involves warming up. We've suggested that athletes go to the gym 20 to 30 minutes before the competition for the team warm-up. The team warm-up should be similar to the practice warm-up. It should consist of a few brief drills or activities that practice skills and include stretching and range-of-motion exercises.

If you are coaching in a youth setting that feeds a high school or club, ask the coaches of those programs for guidance so that your activities complement theirs. The wrestlers can warm up as a group, without partners, with some running, skipping, movement in their stance, and penetration steps. Have them do a few repetitions of large-muscle exercises such as push-ups and crunches. With partners they can work the core muscles by lifting each other in double-leg situations and practicing returning a partner to the mat from behind. When the wrestlers are loose, direct them through drills of takedowns and situations they may encounter. The following are variations for different age groups.

- *Ages 6 to 8*: Use the format just described, but limit drills to the basic techniques you want them to use. Wrestlers this young have very short attention spans, so you have to keep them moving from one thing to the next and make sure they don't wander off.

- *Ages 9 to 10*: These wrestlers will be able to maintain focus a bit longer than their younger friends, but they'll also require a great deal of your attention.

- *Ages 11 to 14*: The 11 to 12 and 13 to 14 age groups are generally better prepared to focus on the warm-up and competition. Use the basic format, but you may have them drill more techniques and situations. The team warm-up might include 15 to 20 minutes of activity, with 5 to 10 minutes for talking to the wrestlers about the day, the skills, and so on.

Finally, you and your wrestlers should know the schedule, and each competitor should plan ahead so that he or she has 10 to 15 minutes (perhaps 10 minutes for 6 to 8 year olds, and 15 minutes for 9 to 14 year olds) before their next match for another warm-up. Wrestlers should do quick large-muscle activities such as push-ups, crunches, and jumping jacks to get the large muscle groups warm, and ideally raise the core body temperature enough to break a light sweat. This sets off some physiological changes that prepare the body for a tough competition. Wrestlers might grab a partner and practice moving in their stance while trying some setups. This should be close enough to the

Coaching Tip
Although the site coordinator and officials have formal responsibility for facilities and equipment, you should know what to look for to ensure that the environment is safe for all wrestlers (see "Facilities and Equipment Checklist" in appendix A on page 176). If you have someone who can help organize the wrestlers for the weigh-in, you might take a few minutes to check the facility, check in with the site coordinator and officials, and then get back to make sure your wrestlers get through the weigh-in procedure alright.

mat they've been called to that they are ready when the previous match ends and can be on the mat and ready to go.

Refrain from delivering long-winded pep talks, but do help athletes mentally prepare for competition by reminding them of the skills they've been working on in recent practices and focusing their attention on what they've been doing well. Remind athletes that they should wrestle hard and smart, practice good sporting behavior, and, above all, have fun.

Unplanned Events

Part of being prepared to coach is to expect the unexpected. What do you do if athletes are late? What if you have an emergency and can't make the match or will be late? What if the match is postponed? Being prepared to handle out-of-the-ordinary circumstances will help you if and when unplanned events occur.

If athletes are late, remind them of the reasons for being on time. First, part of being a team member is being committed to and responsible for the other members. When athletes don't show up or show up late, they break that commitment. Second, if the wrestler misses the weigh-in, his parents, team, and friends may have been inconvenienced for nothing. Once on site and weighed in, athletes need to warm up to physically and mentally prepare for the match. Being late or skipping the warm-up risks injury.

A time may come when an emergency causes you to be late or miss a match. In these cases, notify your assistant coach (if you have one) or your team manager. Also, if notified in advance, another volunteer or a parent of an athlete might be able to step in for the match.

Sometimes a competition must be postponed because of inclement weather or for reasons such as physical problems at the site. If the postponement takes place before the day of the competition, call all team members to let them know. A problem might occur during an all-day tournament, although it is rare. If the weather changes suddenly or a significant physical problem arises at the site and the tournament directors send teams home, gather your team members and explain why the match has been postponed. Make sure that all your athletes have a ride home before you leave—you should be the last to go.

Communicating With Parents

The groundwork for your communication with parents is laid in the parent-orientation meeting, through which parents learn the best ways to support the efforts of their kids (and the whole team). Help parents judge success based not just on the outcome of a match but also on how the kids improve their performances or perhaps just their physical condition.

If parents yell at the kids for their mistakes during a match, make disparaging remarks about the officials or opponents, or shout instructions for which tactics to use, ask them to stop and to instead provide support through their comments and actions. These standards of conduct should be covered in the preseason parent orientation.

When time permits, as parents gather before an event, you can let them know in a general sense what you have been focusing on during the past week and what your goals are for the match. The parents can be a great asset to the coaches and the team by applauding the efforts of the kids on the mat. Their support is especially helpful when the coach has prepped them on what to cheer for in relation to the new techniques and tactics the athletes are learning. Your athletes must come first during this time, however, so focus on the kids during the warm-up.

After a competition, quickly come together as a staff and decide what to say to each wrestler and the team. Then informally assess with parents, as the opportunity arises, how their wrestler did based not on the outcome, but on meeting performance goals and wrestling to the best of his or her ability. Help parents see the competition as a process, not solely as a test that is pass-fail or win-lose. Encourage parents to reinforce that concept at home. For more information on communicating with parents, see page 15 of chapter 2.

During Competition

Throughout the event, you must keep the competition in proper perspective and help your athletes do the same. Observe how your athletes execute skills and how well they support each other. These observations can help you decide appropriate practice plans for the following week. Let's take a more detailed look at your responsibilities during a competition.

Tactical Decisions

Although you may not be called on to create a complex match strategy, you will be called on to make tactical decisions throughout a match. You must decide whether or not to make slight adjustments to your athlete's tactics, and how to deal with wrestlers' performance errors.

Keeping a Proper Perspective

Winning matches is the short-term goal of your wrestling program. The long-term goals are equally important: learning the techniques, tactics, and rules of wrestling; becoming fit; and becoming good sports in wrestling and in life. Most importantly, your young athletes are winning when they are becoming better human beings through their participation in wrestling. You have the privilege of setting the tone for how your wrestlers approach matches. Keep winning and all aspects of the competition in proper perspective, and your young charges will most likely follow suit.

Adjusting Tactics

It is likely that you will make few, if any, tactical adjustments during a match, especially for younger age groups. It is far more important for your athletes to focus on properly executing the tactics you have taught them during practice than on making adjustments during a match. However, if adjustments must be made, make only minor changes that fall within the scope of what the athletes have already learned. Consider the following questions when adjusting team tactics:

- How does your opponent usually initiate attacks? Do wrestlers from an opposing club or team consistently attack a certain way, such as using upper-body techniques or rolls from the bottom?

- Are certain opponents less conditioned so that the longer a match goes, the more they will tire?

Determining the answers to such questions can help you formulate an effective match plan and make proper adjustments as the match progresses. However, don't stress tactics too much during a match. Doing so can take the fun out of the match for the athletes. If you don't trust your memory, carry a pen and pad to note which individual skills need attention at the next practice.

Correcting Athletes' Errors

In chapter 6 you learned about two types of errors: learning errors and performance errors. Learning errors are those that occur because athletes don't know how to perform a skill. Performance errors are made not because athletes don't know how to execute the skill, but because they make mistakes in carrying out what they do know.

Sometimes it's not easy to tell which type of error athletes are making. Knowing your athletes' capabilities helps you to determine whether they know the skill and are simply making mistakes in executing it or whether they don't know how to perform it. If they are making learning errors, note the problem and cover it at the next practice. Match time is not the time to teach skills.

If your wrestlers are making performance errors, however, you can help correct them during a match. Athletes who make performance errors often do so because they have a lapse in concentration or motivation, or they are simply demonstrating human error. Competition can also adversely affect a young athlete's technique, and a word of encouragement about concentration may help. If you do correct a performance error during a match, do so in a quiet, controlled, and positive tone of voice, either during a break or when the athlete is with you off the mat. Try not to work with a wrestler this way when others are paying attention.

When athletes make performance errors, you must determine whether the error is an occasional error that anyone can make or whether the error is expected at a particular stage of development. If the error is expected, then the athlete may appreciate your not commenting; he or she knows it was a mistake and may already know how to correct it. On the other hand, perhaps an encouraging word and a coaching cue such as "Remember to keep your elbows in!" are just what the athlete needs. Knowing your athletes and judging what to say are essential parts of the art of coaching.

Coach and Athlete Behavior

Another aspect of coaching on match day is managing behavior—your athletes' and your own. Being composed and focused during a match is crucial to good performance by both the athletes and the coaches.

Coach Conduct

You greatly influence your athletes' behavior before, during, and after a match. If you're up, your athletes are more likely to be up. If you're anxious, they'll take notice, and the anxiety can become contagious. If you're negative, they'll respond with worry. If you're positive, they'll compete with more enjoyment. If you're constantly yelling instructions or commenting on mistakes, it will be difficult for athletes to concentrate.

Focus on positive competition and on having a good time. Let athletes get into the flow of the match. A coach who overorganizes everything and dominates a match from the corner is definitely not making the contest fun. So how should you conduct yourself? Here are a few pointers:

- Be calm, in control, and supportive of your athletes.
- Encourage athletes often, but instruct sparingly. Athletes should focus on their performance, not on directions shouted from the corner.
- If you need to instruct an athlete, do so when he or she is off the mat, and do so in an unobtrusive manner. Never yell at athletes for making a mistake. Instead, briefly demonstrate or remind them of the correct technique and then encourage them. Tell them how to correct the problem on the mat.

Make certain that you have discussed coaching demeanor as a staff and that everyone is in agreement about the way they will conduct themselves—then stick with it. Remember, your athletes are not competing for an Olympic gold medal. In this program, wrestling competitions are designed to help athletes develop their skills and character and have fun. So coach matches in a manner that helps your athletes achieve these goals.

Athlete Conduct

It is the responsibility of coaches and parents to teach appropriate sporting behavior and to keep athletes under control. Do so by setting a good example and disciplining when necessary. Set team rules for good behavior. If athletes attempt to cheat, fight, argue, badger, yell disparaging remarks, and so forth, it is your responsibility to correct the misbehavior. Explain that their behavior is not acceptable for your team and that if they want to wrestle, they must not repeat the action.

Consider team rules in these areas of match conduct:

- Athlete language
- Athlete behavior
- Interactions with officials
- Discipline for misbehavior
- Dress code for matches

Athlete Welfare

All athletes are not the same. Some attach their self-worth to winning and losing. This idea is fueled by coaches, parents, peers, and society, who place great emphasis on winning. Athletes become anxious when they're uncertain whether they can meet the expectations of others—especially when meeting a particular expectation is important to them also.

If your athletes look uptight and anxious during a competition, find ways to ease their worries about their performance and to reduce the importance they are attaching to the match. Help athletes focus on realistic personal goals that are attainable and measurable and that will help them improve their performance while they have fun. Another way to reduce anxiety on match day is to stay away from emotional prematch pep talks. Instead, remind athletes of the techniques and tactics they will use and encourage them to wrestle hard, do their best, and have fun.

When coaching during matches, remember that the most important outcome from wrestling is each athlete's increased self-worth. Keep that objective firmly in mind and strive to promote it through every coaching decision.

Opponents and Officials

Respect opponents and officials because without them, there wouldn't be a competition. Opponents provide opportunities for your athletes to test themselves, improve, and excel. Officials help provide a fair and safe experience for athletes and can help them gain a better understanding of the sport.

Keeping the Competition Safe

Chapter 4 is devoted to athlete safety, but it's worth noting here that safety during matches can be affected by how officials call the rules. If officials don't call rules correctly and thus risk injury to your athletes, you must intervene. Voice your concern in a respectful manner that places the emphasis where it should be: on the athletes' safety. One of the officials' main responsibilities is to look after everyone's safety, and they should work with coaches to protect the athletes as much as possible. Don't hesitate to address a safety issue with an official when the need arises.

You and your athletes should show respect for opponents and officials by being polite and putting forth your best efforts. Don't allow your athletes to trash-talk or taunt an opponent or an official. Such behavior is disrespectful to the spirit of the competition, and you should immediately remove an athlete from a match if he or she disobeys your team rules in this area.

Remember, too, that officials at this level might be teenagers—in many cases not much older than the athletes themselves—and that the level of officiating should be commensurate with the level of competition. In other words, don't expect perfection from officials any more than you do from your own athletes. As long as the officials are making calls consistently on both sides and addressing the penalties, most of your officiating concerns will be met.

After the Competition

When the match is over, join your team in congratulating the coaches and athletes of the opposing team, and then be sure to thank the officials. Bring athletes together to cool-down briefly and to replenish fluids. Check on injuries and inform athletes how to care for them. Be prepared to speak with the officials about problems that occurred during the match. Then hold a brief meeting to ensure that your athletes are on an even keel, whether they won or lost.

Coaching Tip
The total time from the start of the cool-down to the conclusion of the postmatch meeting should be approximately 2 minutes for the 6 to 8 age group, increasing with older groups to a maximum of 10 minutes for the 13 to 14 age group.

Reactions After a Competition

Your first concern after a match should be your athletes' attitudes and mental well-being. You don't want them to be too high after a win or too low after a loss. After a match is when you can most influence them to keep the outcome in perspective and settle their feelings.

When celebrating a victory, make sure your athletes do so in a way that doesn't show disrespect for the opponents. It's appropriate to be happy about a win, but don't allow your athletes to taunt an opponent or boast about their victory. If they've lost, your athletes will naturally be disappointed. But if they've made a winning effort, let them know it. Help them be proud and maintain a positive attitude that will carry over to the next practice and competition. Winning and losing are a part of life, not just a part of sport. If athletes learn to handle both well, they'll have a skill they can apply to whatever they do.

Postcompetition Team Meeting

After the competition, gather your team in a designated area for a short meeting. Before this meeting, decide as a staff what to say and who will say it. Be sure that the staff speaks with one voice.

If your wrestlers have performed well, compliment and congratulate them. Whether they've won or lost, tell them specifically what they did with proficiency. Such commendation will reinforce their desire to repeat their good performances. Don't use this time to criticize individual performances or dwell on tactical problems. You should help wrestlers improve their skills, but do so at the next practice—they won't absorb much tactical information immediately after a competition.

Finally, make sure your wrestlers have transportation home. Be the last one to leave to ensure full supervision of your wrestlers.

11

Developing Season and Practice Plans

We hope you've learned a lot from this book: what your responsibilities are as a coach, how to communicate well and provide for safety, how to teach and shape skills, and how to coach competitions. But competitions make up only a portion of your season—you and your wrestlers will spend more time in practices than in competition. How well you conduct practices and prepare your wrestlers for competition will greatly affect not only your wrestlers' enjoyment and success throughout the season but also your own.

Fun Learning Environment

Regardless of which phase of your season you are in, work to create an environment that welcomes learning and promotes teamwork. Following are seven tips to help you and your staff get the most out of your practices:

1. Stick to the practice times agreed on as a staff.
2. Start and end each practice as a team.
3. Keep the practice routine as consistent as possible so that the wrestlers can feel comfortable.
4. Be organized in your approach by moving quickly from one activity to another and from one stage of training to another.
5. Tell your wrestlers what the practice will include before the practice starts.
6. Allow the wrestlers to take water breaks whenever needed.
7. Focus on providing positive feedback.

You may also want to consider using wrestling activities to add variety and make practices more fun. In appendix C on page 185, you will find 23 wrestling activities. Performing these activities in each practice prepares wrestlers for the many different situations that arise during competitions.

Season Plans

Your season plan is a snapshot of the entire season. Before the first practice with your wrestlers, you must sit down as a staff and develop this plan. To do so, simply write down each practice and competition date on a calendar and then go back and number the practices. These practice numbers are the foundation of your season plan. Now you can work through the plan, moving from practice to practice, and outline what you hope to cover in each practice by noting the purpose of the practice, the main skills you will cover, and the activities you will use.

The following table contains more detailed information about the objectives you should consider as you build your plans for particular age groups.

Objective	Skills
To learn motion in proper stance (ages <8-14)	Stance, position, motion
To learn motion in a stance with contact and tie-ups (ages <8-14)	Stance, position, motion
To learn basic ways to attack an opponent's hips (ages <8-14)	Stance, level change, double-leg penetration, single-leg penetration
To learn basic breakdown skills (ages <8-14)	Mat position, balance, applying force properly, timing
To learn proper technique in finishing takedowns (ages <8-14)	Lifting from a double leg, completing the single-leg takedown
To practice facing an opponent when out of a good stance while the attacker practices scoring a go-behind (ages <8-14)	Motion, level change
To learn hip movement from the bottom position (ages <8-14)	Gaining separation between the hips, hip-heist, sit-out
To learn ways to reverse control of an opponent (ages <8-14)	Hip-heist
To learn ways to pin an opponent for a fall (ages <8-14)	Breakdown, pressure, half nelson, bar arm
To learn proper technique for throws, to take an opponent from the feet to the back—headlock for ages 8 and younger; add reverse headlock for ages 9-10; add hip toss for ages 11-14	Motion, level change, back step, back arch
To learn the motion associated with common wrestling situations (ages <8-14)	Stance (square or staggered), sprawl, movement to set up takedowns
To learn the correct starting position for top and bottom (ages <8-14)	Proper body position for various techniques
To learn more advanced ways to pin a defender for the fall (ages 9-14)	Half nelson, bar arms, chicken wing
To practice snapping and moving an opponent in a head tie (ages 9-14)	Motion, level change
To examine the techniques used in throwing and countering a headlock—sag headlock for offense and countering techniques for defense (ages 9-14)	Motion, level change, back step, back arch
To understand how to counter a sprawl with the opponent in a front headlock position (ages 9-14)	Motion, level change, backing out safely
To learn the whizzer as a way to control the opponent's motion (ages 9-14)	Motion, level change, penetration, lifting
To learn the skills of taking an opponent to the back from a low-level or front headlock position (ages 9-14)	Motion, level change, position
To learn basic maneuvers to score from a sitting position (ages 9-14)	Hip-heist, turn-in and stand-up, head shrug
To learn more advanced ways of taking down an opponent (ages 11-14)	High-crotch takedown, low-single takedown
To learn more advanced ways of moving an opponent from a head tie (ages 11-14)	Movement, penetration, snap down
To learn an advanced way of putting a person on the back from both the top position and the neutral position (ages 13-14)	Turk step
To learn advanced ways of turning an opponent with a leg ride (ages 13-14)	Crossface into a turk

Coaching Tip

While developing your season plan, keep in mind that you will want to incorporate the games approach into your practices. The games approach can be superior to the traditional approach because it focuses on replicating the competitive environment. Using matchlike activities better prepares athletes, both physically and mentally, for the demands of a match.

The appropriate age range is listed for each objective. When you have laid out and numbered your practices, assign these objectives to various practices, making sure you have introduced them all before competition begins. Try to cover each of the basic aspects—takedowns, top position, and bottom position—at each practice. Simply practicing to achieve any one of the objectives will leave too much ground uncovered in a short season.

Season Plan for Ages 8 and Under

Many children 8 years old and younger have had little or no exposure to wrestling. Assume that these children have no knowledge of the sport. Throughout the season, wrestlers in this age group need to work on several things: the importance of fair play and good sportsmanship, the basic concepts of the sport, fitness and strength, and an understanding of and ability to use power.

Wrestlers that are 8 years old and younger need to learn, and learn to apply, basic skills along with the following concepts during their season. They need to learn proper stance and body position on their feet, how to move in their stance in order to score a takedown, how to move in stance and sprawl to avoid being taken down, how to complete takedowns and gain control on the mat, how to ride and break down the bottom wrestler when both are on the mat, how to turn the bottom wrestler over to get the near fall or pin, and how to escape or achieve a reversal from the bottom position.

On the feet, these young wrestlers should learn the single-leg and double-leg takedowns, the headlock, and the sprawl for a go-behind. They must learn to lift an opponent they have gotten behind, or who has tried a stand-up escape, and return the wrestler to the mat. They must learn the stand-up, hip-heist, and switch so that they can escape or reverse the control when they are in the bottom position. Also in the bottom position, young wrestlers need to learn to fight off a half nelson. When they are in the top position on the mat, they should learn the outside ankle breakdown and the inside ankle breakdown. Also in the top position, they must learn the half nelson in combination with a bar arm.

Season Plan for Ages 9 to 10

Wrestlers who are 9 to 10 years old with two years or more of experience will continue to learn and refine the basic skills and concepts they have already learned. These are proper stance and body position on their feet, how to move in their stance in order to score a takedown, how to move in stance and sprawl to avoid being taken down, how to complete takedowns and gain control on the mat, how to ride and break down the bottom wrestler when both are on the mat, how to turn the bottom wrestler over to get the near fall or pin, and how to escape or achieve a reversal from the bottom position.

On the feet, these young wrestlers should refine the single-leg and double-leg takedowns, the headlock, and the sprawl for the go-behind that they learned earlier. The reverse headlock should be added for situations when the headlock is resisted. They must continue to work on lifting an opponent they have gotten behind, or who has tried a stand-up escape, and returning the wrestler to the mat. They must work on stand-ups, hip-heists, and switches from new situations so that they can escape or reverse the control of more advanced wrestlers when they are in the bottom position.

In the bottom position, young wrestlers need to learn to work actively to break the top person's attempts to turn them to their back, and to think about their escape and reversal attempts as offensive efforts. When they are in the top position on the mat, they should start working on the spiral ride and refine the outside ankle breakdown and the inside ankle breakdown that they have already learned. Also in the top position, they must continue to work on the half nelson in combination with a bar arm and add the chicken wing with the half nelson.

Wrestlers in the 9 to 10 age group who have little or no experience should work through a season plan for wrestlers 8 and younger. You should learn to recognize when these older wrestlers are ready to move up to another practice grouping. Older beginners may move through the basics quickly, or they may have some bad habits to overcome. Each will move at his or her own pace.

Throughout the season, these wrestlers should continue to work on several things: the importance of fair play and good sportsmanship, the basic concepts of the sport, fitness and strength, and an understanding of and the use of power. Make sure that the wrestlers are having fun. It is easy to become too focused on the plan—without fun you may end up with a small group at the end of the season.

Season Plan for Ages 11 to 12

Wrestlers who are 11 to 12 years old with two to four years of experience will continue to learn and refine the skills and concepts they have already learned. These are proper stance and body position on their feet, how to move in their stance and penetrate to be able to get a takedown, how to move in stance and sprawl to avoid being taken down, how to complete takedowns and gain control on the mat, how to ride and break down the bottom wrestler when both are on the mat, how to turn the bottom wrestler over to get the near fall or pin, and how to escape or achieve a reversal from the bottom position.

These wrestlers will continue to refine the single-leg and double-leg takedowns, the headlock and reverse headlock, and the sprawl for a go-behind. The elbow shuck should be introduced along with the high crotch, and these should be learned in combination.

Wrestlers at all levels must continue to work on lifting an opponent they have gotten behind, or who has tried a stand-up escape, and returning the wrestler to the mat. They must continue to work on stand-ups, hip-heists, and switches, exploring new situations and timing. All young wrestlers need to learn to work actively to break the top person's attempts to turn them to their back, and to think about their escape and reversal attempts as offensive efforts. When wrestlers are in the top position on the mat, they must refine the outside ankle breakdown, the inside ankle breakdown, and the spiral ride that they have already learned. They must continue to work on the half nelson in combination with a bar arm, and the chicken wing with the half nelson. The wrestlers can start to explore rolling with these pinning combinations as discussed in chapter 9.

Season Plan for Ages 13 to 14

Wrestlers 13 to 14 years old with several years of experience will, like wrestlers at all levels, continue to learn and refine the skills and concepts they have already learned.

More experienced wrestlers will want to move to more advanced techniques, which can be more fun. But it is as important for them to go over the basics and work through them at the start of a season as it is for the 8-year-olds.

Working on proper stance and body position; moving in their stance to score; and working on stance, movement, and the sprawl to avoid being taken down all contribute to mental preparation for the season. These activities also work the muscle groups that need to be conditioned and built for the season. Skipping these steps at the start of the season leaves wrestlers with an inadequate foundation. Similarly, they must work through finishing the takedowns they already know, riding and breakdowns, pinning combinations, and escapes and reversals from the bottom position.

The basics on the mat are important, too. Wrestlers must continue to work on lifting and returning opponents to the mat and explore the breakdowns and pinning combinations they know, trying new applications. From the bottom position they must continue to work on stand-ups, hip-heists, and switches, exploring new starting positions, situations, and timing. This is a great age to begin work on the leg rides and the new combinations they lead to. Again, work to assure that practices are fun as well as hard work.

Practice Plans

Coaches rarely believe they have enough time to practice everything they want to cover. Therefore, practice plans help you organize your thoughts so that you stay on track to reach your practice objectives and help you better visualize and prepare so that you can run your practices effectively.

First and foremost, your practice plans should be appropriate for the age group you are coaching. It is common for coaches of young wrestlers to have a full range of ages in the practice setting at the same time. As you have seen, the basics must be included in the season plan for all age groups—all the way up through Olympians, in fact. This makes it possible for multiple age groups to practice in the same session to some extent. If you are in this situation, it can be beneficial for the more experienced wrestlers to help the young people figure out the basics. This helps build camaraderie, but more important, teaching a younger wrestler may be the best way to help the teacher to truly learn a technique or concept.

Each practice plan should include a warm-up and cool-down. During the cool-down, coaches should attend to any injuries suffered during practice and make sure that the athletes drink plenty of water.

Constructing practice plans requires both organization and flexibility on your part. Don't be intimidated by the amount of material you've listed in your season plan that you want to cover. Pick out a few basics and build your initial practice plans around them; this process will get easier after you've drafted a few plans. Then you can move from teaching simple concepts and skills to drawing up plans that introduce more complex ones. Build in flexibility; if you find that what you've planned for practice isn't working, have a backup activity that approaches the skill or concept from a different angle. The priorities are to keep your athletes wrestling and to help everyone have fun while they're learning.

Sample Practice Plan for Ages 8 and Under

Activity	Description	Coaching Points
Warm-up (10 min.)	3-5 min.—Athletes jog around the perimeter of the wrestling mats. 15-20 crunches—Work up to 30 over the first weeks (knees up, arms crossed on chest—don't allow the wrestlers to pull on their necks). 5-15 push-ups (depending on ability)—Build up to 15-25 over time; it is fine to do these from the knees until strength is built. Static stretching—Stretch low back and legs.	• The warm-up increases circulation and loosens joints. • The warm-up prepares the body for more vigorous exercise.
Stance (11 min.)	3 min.—Demonstrate stance, emphasizing concepts such as placement of the center of gravity, head position, and hand and arm position. 3 min.—Discuss the reasons that the position of the body, head, and arms is important. 3-5 min.—Work with the wrestlers as they practice their stances.	• Remind wrestlers to keep the head up—it's easier to stay in control of yourself. • With the head down, it's easier for the other person to establish control. • With the head up, a shot goes straight at the opponent. • With the head down, the shot will go straight down.

(continued)

Sample Practice Plan for Ages 8 and Under *(continued)*

Activity	Description	Coaching Points
Movement (12 min.)	3 min.—Demonstrate movement in stance, forward, backward, and to each side. 3 min.—Have the wrestlers explore movement on their own. 3 min.—Have the wrestlers move in a direction you call out for a few seconds between changes. 3 min.—Stop and discuss what you have observed. Have someone that is doing well demonstrate. It can be good to have others emulate a few people who are doing well.	• Emphasize smooth movements. • Watch for positions—praise good and make positive suggestions such as, "Your center of gravity is just right—if you bring your head up, a shot will work better." • If you see people crossing their feet or making another mistake, have them watch you or watch another wrestler, and emphasize what they are doing well that others should copy.
Level change (12 min.)	3 min.—Bring the group together to discuss why changing levels is important, demonstrating as you do. 3 min.—Have the wrestlers practice making level changes while staying in their stances. 3 min.—Have the wrestlers move in their stance, changing directions on your call and making level changes on your call. 3 min.—Bring the wrestlers together to discuss what you've seen and make suggestions.	• Emphasize position—body, head, and arms. • Emphasize smooth motion and keeping the head up.
Penetration step (12 min.)	3 min.—Bring the group together to discuss the concept of penetration and demonstrate the penetration step. 3 min.—Have the wrestlers assume their stance without partners. On your call, have them make the level change and then the penetration step back up to their stance. 3 min.—Bring the group back together and talk about what you observed and make positive comments. 3 min.—From their stance and with the motion that you direct, have the wrestlers make the level change and penetration step on your call.	• Emphasize the concept of the attacking wrestler moving all the way through the defender. • Two things can't be in the same space at the same time. • Talk about imagining that there is an opponent in front of each of the wrestlers, and have them think about penetrating from an angle.
Fun time (10 min.)	You have just presented a ton of information to young kids, so now let them relax and have some fun. Organize a group game that has a conditioning aspect to it.	• In the early part of the season, assume that the wrestlers are not ready to actually wrestle. Instead, you should substitute a fun activity.
Cool-down (10 min.)	3-5 min.—Athletes jog around the mats and then stretch as a team. 5 min.—Have wrestlers talk about the things they've learned, emphasizing the concepts more than the technique.	• Lower heart rate and body temperature gradually. • Improve flexibility.

Sample Practice Plan for Ages 9 to 10

Activity	Description	Coaching Points
Warm-up (10 min.)	3-5 min.—Athletes jog around the perimeter of the wrestling mats. 15-20 crunches—Work up to 30 over the first weeks (knees up, arms crossed on chest—don't allow the wrestlers to pull on their necks). 5-15 push-ups (depending on ability)—Build up to 15-25 over time; it is fine to do these from the knees until strength is built. 10-15 penetration steps—Build up to 15-25. The group is in their stance and moving in the same direction in the circle. Wrestlers change direction twice on your call, then do a full level change and penetration step, coming back up into their stance. Static stretching—Stretch low back and legs.	• The warm-up increases circulation and loosens joints. • The warm-up prepares the body for more vigorous exercise. • Emphasize the importance of the warm-up—especially for competition. Many wrestlers think they will get tired, when in fact, a good warm-up ensures that they will tire less quickly in competition.
Bottom position—specific moves (11 min.)	3 min.—Demonstrate proper bottom starting position, talking about how the wrestlers might position themselves to be able to do certain moves. Emphasize concepts such as trying to have the weight as elevated as possible for stand-ups, or forward for hip-heists or sit-outs, and so on. 3 min.—Have the wrestlers assume their bottom position and ask them to shift around as necessary to do various moves that you call out. 3-5 min.—From their stance, with no one on top, have the wrestlers assume the stance for the move you call, then have them execute the move on the whistle.	• Wrestlers should have little or no weight on the hands for stand-ups. • The head should be up and the eyes on the official when in the starting position. • Look for good movement and positions that will create space between the two wrestlers' hips.
Top position—specific moves (13 min.)	3 min.—Bring the wrestlers together and have them think about how they would counter what they just worked on if they were on top; solicit ideas from the athletes and add to these. 3 min.—Partner the wrestlers and have one assume the bottom position. Have the other assume the basic top starting position. Ask, "What will you do if you know a team always does the stand-up? What will you do if they try to use a switch or a hip-heist? What kind of breakdown, and therefore starting position, will help you take away the bottom wrestler's element of surprise?" Have them work through each of these on their own, asking questions of you or others as they explore. 5-7 min.—Using little resistance and maybe half speed, have the bottom wrestler assume his or her stance and have the top wrestler come on. On your call, have them do a start.	• Emphasize smooth movements. • Watch for positions—praise good, and make positive suggestions such as, "Your starting position was good. If you keep your head up when you do the stand-up, your upper body will come up better." • Feel how the positions affect what happens.

Sample Practice Plan for Ages 9 to 10 *(continued)*

Activity	Description	Coaching Points
Single leg from an angle (16 min.)	3 min.—Bring the group together to discuss why attacking from an angle is important, demonstrating as you do. 3 min.—Have the wrestlers assume their stance and move as if an opponent is in front of them, thinking all the time about getting an angle. 5-7 min.—Partner the wrestlers and have both assume their stance. One will be still, the other moving in his or her stance. Have them change level, do a penetration step, and complete the single leg when they feel they have the correct angle. Have each one do several repetitions. 3 min.—Bring the wrestlers together to discuss what you've seen. Ask if anyone can talk about what they feel the angle does, and make suggestions.	• Emphasize position—body, head, and arms. • Emphasize smooth motion and keeping the head up. • Emphasize the concept of the attacking wrestler moving all the way through the space the defender was in. • Point out that attacking from the angle forces the opponent's weight onto the far foot, making it tougher to sprawl.
Movement in stance—sprawl on a shot (19 min.)	2-3 min.—Bring the group together to discuss how they'll recognize when a shot is developing. 3 min.—Have the wrestlers assume their stance without partners. Have them face the same way and move in different directions on your call. On a subtle signal, have them make their own level change and sprawl, catching their weight on their hands with extended arms. They should come right back up into their stance. 3 min.—Bring the group back together and talk about what you observed, making positive comments. Note that with a wrestler in front of them, the signal will be different—the start of a level change, maybe a change in breathing, it could be anything. 5-7 min.—Partner the wrestlers and have them moving in their stance, working to get an angle. One partner will be the attacker and the other the defender. Every time the attacker gets the right angle, he or she should make a level change and penetrate. The defender must recognize the initiation and make the sprawl. Alternate so that each performs the same number of repetitions. 3 min.—Bring the group back together to talk about what worked and what didn't. Share your observations and answer questions.	• Have the wrestlers watch the opponent's midsection; if it begins to drop, a level change is starting. • When wrestlers are moving, make sure they do not circle into the opponent's lead leg—the one he or she will penetrate with. This shortens the distance for the attacker. • Talk about imagining an opponent in front of each wrestler and have them think about penetrating from an angle.
Cool-down (10 min.)	3-5 min.—Athletes jog around the mats and then stretch as a team. 5 min.—Have wrestlers talk about the things they've learned, emphasizing the concepts more than the technique.	• Lower heart rate and body temperature gradually. • Improve flexibility.

Sample Practice Plan for Ages 11 to 12

Activity	Description	Coaching Points
Warm-up (10 min.)	3-5 min.—Athletes jog around the perimeter of the wrestling mats. 15-20 crunches—Work up to 30 over the first weeks (knees up, arms crossed on chest—don't allow the wrestlers to pull on their necks). 5-15 push-ups (depending on ability)—Build up to 15-25 over time; it is fine to do these from the knees until strength is built. 10-15 penetration steps—Build up to 15-25. The group is in their stance and moving in the same direction in the circle. Wrestlers change direction twice on your call, then do a full level change and penetration step, coming back up into their stance. Static stretching—Stretch low back and legs.	• The warm-up increases circulation and loosens joints. • The warm-up prepares the body for more vigorous exercise. • Emphasize the importance of the warm-up—especially for competition. Many wrestlers think they will get tired, when in fact a good warm-up ensures that they will tire less quickly in competition.
Stance, tie-ups, movement (31 min.)	3 min.—Demonstrate proper stance and head position, then go through the basic tie-ups. 7-9 min.—Partner the wrestlers. Have them get in their stance and practice initiating these tie-ups. 3 min.—With good tie-ups, demonstrate how to move the opponent into position for a takedown attempt. 7-9 min.—At half speed and with little resistance, have the wrestlers explore moving their opponent with effective tie-ups and motion. 5-7 min.—Again at half speed and with little resistance, have the partners take turns initiating the tie-up, moving the opponent, and initiating and completing the takedown attempts of their choice.	• Have wrestlers go forehead to forehead or position the forehead on the opponent's temple. • Remind wrestlers to keep the head up. If the head is up, the opponent's collar tie will be ineffective. • Emphasize that the tie-up must come from the inside—with low hands in good stance. • Emphasize the idea of using the tie-up to bring the opponent with them when they move—the arms don't pull; the whole body, working together, moves. • Keep a close eye on the level of cooperation—young wrestlers may feel like they have to "win" even these situations.
Top position—specific moves (10 min.)	3 min.—Bring the wrestlers together and demonstrate three or four variations of breakdowns, emphasizing the basic concepts. 5-7 min.—Have the wrestlers partner and take turns being up and down. On your call (for the start and the technique) have them work through all of the techniques. The bottom wrestler does nothing. After the first few, call the technique and have them start on the whistle.	• Emphasize coming up off the knees to make the defender carry all the weight. • Take a minute to explain ways to be moving at the whistle, especially watching the official's lips around the whistle. When they tighten to blow, it is often safe to go rather than waiting to actually hear the signal. This takes practice, and officials vary. • This is just to feel how the positions affect what happens.

(continued)

Sample Practice Plan for Ages 11 to 12 *(continued)*

Activity	Description	Coaching Points
Single leg from an angle (16 min.)	3 min.—Bring the group together to discuss why attacking from an angle is important, demonstrating as you do. 3 min.—Have the wrestlers assume their stance and move as if an opponent is in front of them, thinking all the time about getting an angle. 5-7 min.—Partner the wrestlers and have both assume their stance. One will be still, the other moving in the stance. Have them change levels, make a penetration step, and complete the single leg when they feel they have the correct angle. Have each wrestler do several repetitions. 3 min.—Bring the wrestlers together to discuss what you've seen. Ask if anyone can talk about what they feel the angle does, and make suggestions.	• Emphasize position—body, head, and arms. • Emphasize smooth motion and keeping the head up. • Emphasize the concept of the attacking wrestler moving all the way through the space the defender was in.
Movement in stance— sprawl on a shot (19 min.)	2-3 min.—Bring the group together to discuss how they'll recognize when a shot is developing. 3 min.—Have the wrestlers assume their stance without partners. Have them face the same way and move in different directions on your call. On a subtle signal, have them make their own level change and sprawl, catching their weight on their hands with extended arms. They should come right back up into their stance. 3 min.—Bring the group back together and talk about what you observed and make positive comments. Note that with a wrestler in front of them, the signal will be different— the start of a level change, maybe a change in breathing, it could be anything. 5-7 min.—Partner the wrestlers. Have them both move in their stance, working to get an angle. One will be the attacker, the other the defender. Every time the attacker gets the right angle, he or she should change level and penetrate. The defender must recognize the initiation and make the sprawl. Alternate so that each performs the same number of repetitions. 3 min.—Bring the group back together to talk about what worked and what didn't. Share your observations and answer questions.	• Have the wrestlers watch the opponent's midsection; if it starts to drop, a level change is starting. • When wrestlers are moving, make sure they do not circle into the opponent's lead leg—the one he or she will penetrate with. This shortens the distance for the attacker. • Talk about imagining an opponent in front of each wrestler and have the wrestlers think about penetrating from an angle.
Cool-down (10 min.)	3-5 min.—Athletes jog around the mats and then stretch as a team. 5 min.—Have wrestlers talk about the things they've learned, emphasizing the concepts more than the technique.	• Lower heart rate and body temperature gradually. • Improve flexibility. • Remarkable examples will help young kids remember; yelling will *not* help kids remember.

Sample Practice Plan for Ages 13 to 14

Activity	Description	Coaching Points
Warm-up (10 min.)	3-5 min.—Athletes jog around the perimeter of the wrestling mats. 15-20 crunches—Work up to 30 over the first weeks (knees up, arms crossed on chest—don't allow the wrestlers to pull on their necks). 5-15 push-ups (depending on ability)—Build up to 15-25 over time; it is fine to do these from the knees until strength is built. 10-15 penetration steps—Build up to 15-25. The group is in their stance and moving in the same direction in the circle. Wrestlers change direction twice on your call, then do a full level change and penetration step, coming back up into their stance. Static stretching—Stretch low back and legs.	• The warm-up increases circulation and loosens joints. • The warm-up prepares the body for more vigorous exercise. • Emphasize the importance of the warm-up—especially for competition. Many wrestlers think they will get tired, when in fact a good warm-up ensures that they will tire less quickly in competition.
Bottom position—stand-up escapes (11 min.)	3 min.—Demonstrate proper bottom starting position for stand-ups, talking about how the wrestlers might position themselves to be able to do them if the top wrestler is on one side or the other. Emphasize trying to have the weight as elevated as possible so there is less distance to the standing position. 3 min.—Have the wrestlers assume their bottom position and have them work on developing explosive movement with the arms driving into the mat to start the head and body coming up. 3-5 min.—From the bottom position, with no one on top, have the wrestlers assume the stance for the stand-up that you call, then have them execute the move on the whistle.	• Remind wrestlers to put little or no weight on the hands for stand-ups. • Emphasize keeping the head up in the starting position and eyes on the official. • Look for good movement and positions that will create space between the two wrestlers' hips. • Watch for positions—praise good and make positive suggestions, such as "Your starting position was good; if you keep your head up when you do the stand-up, your upper body will come up better."
Top position—adapting to counter bottom moves (13 min.)	3 min.—Bring the wrestlers together and have them think about how they would counter what they just worked on if they were on top; solicit ideas from the athletes and add to these. 3 min.—Partner the wrestlers and have one assume the bottom position. Have the other assume the basic top starting position. Ask, "What will you do if you know a team always does a stand-up? What will you do if they try to use a switch or a hip-heist? What kind of breakdown, and therefore starting position, will help you take away the bottom wrestler's element of surprise?" Have them work through each of these on their own, asking questions of you or others as they explore. 5-7 min.—Using little resistance and maybe half speed, have the bottom wrestler assume his or her stance, have the top wrestler come on, and on your call, have them do a start.	• Emphasize smooth movements. • Remind wrestlers to have a game plan before the action starts. • Praise the bottom wrestler for giving the proper amount of resistance to the top wrestler's moves. • Offer specific positive feedback to wrestlers who are doing moves correctly (e.g., "Great job grabbing the ankle to stop the stand-up!")

(continued)

Sample Practice Plan for Ages 13 to 14 *(continued)*

Activity	Description	Coaching Points
Elbow shuck— using the elbow shuck to set up the high crotch (18 min.)	3 min.—Bring the group together to discuss how various tie-ups can be countered. Emphasize the idea of using the opponent's collar tie attempt against him or her with the elbow shuck. 5 min.—From a good stance but with little resistance, have one wrestler initiate a collar tie and the other tie up on the elbow of the arm that's on the neck, circle into that side, and with the head up, drive the elbow straight across and into the opponent's chest. Switch and repeat several times. 5-7 min.—Partner the wrestlers and have both assume their stance. One will have a collar tie, the other a tie on that elbow. The wrestler with the elbow will circle into that side, shuck the elbow, and finish the takedown as either a single-leg takedown or a go-behind. Have wrestlers switch and repeat. 3 min.—Bring the wrestlers together to discuss what you've seen. Ask if anyone can talk about why creating angles is advantageous, and give suggestions.	• Emphasize position— body, head, and arms. • Emphasize smooth motion and keeping the head up. • Emphasize the concept of the attacking wrestler moving all the way through the space the defender was in. • Emphasize keeping the head up, changing levels, and penetrating. • Call attention to the defender's weight being shifted to the far foot, preventing a sprawl.
Movement in stance— sprawl on a shot (19 min.)	2-3 min.—Bring the group together to discuss how they'll recognize when a shot is developing. 3 min.—Have the wrestlers assume their stance without partners. Have them face the same way and move in different directions on your call. On a subtle signal, have them make their own level change and sprawl, catching their weight on their hands with extended arms. They should come right back up into their stance. 3 min.—Bring the group back together and talk about what you observed and make positive comments. Note that with a wrestler in front of them, the signal will be different—the start of a level change, maybe a change in breathing, it could be anything. 5-7 min.—Partner the wrestlers. Have them both move in their stance, working to get an angle. One will be the attacker, the other the defender. Every time the attacker gets the right angle, he or she should change level and penetrate. The defender must recognize the initiation and make the sprawl. Alternate so that each performs the same number of repetitions. 3 min.—Bring the group back together to talk about what worked and what didn't. Share your observations and answer questions.	• Have wrestlers watch the opponent's midsection; if it starts to drop, a level change is starting. • When moving, make sure wrestlers do not circle into the opponent's lead leg—the one he or she will penetrate with. This shortens the distance for the attacker. • Talk about imagining an opponent in front of each wrestler and have them think about penetrating from an angle.
Cool-down (10 min.)	3-5 min.—Athletes jog around the mats and then stretch as a team. 5 min.—Have wrestlers talk about the things they've learned, emphasizing the concepts more than the technique.	• Lower heart rate and body temperature gradually. • Improve flexibility.

Appendix A

Related Checklists and Forms

This appendix contains all checklists and forms mentioned in the text. You may reproduce and use them as needed for your wrestling program.

Facilities and Equipment Checklist

☐ The stairs and corridors leading to the gym or wrestling room are well lit.

☐ The stairs and corridors are free of obstruction.

☐ The stairs and corridors are in good repair.

☐ Exits are well marked and illuminated.

☐ Exits are free of obstruction.

☐ Uprights and other projections are padded.

☐ Walls are free of projections.

☐ Windows are located high on the walls.

☐ Wall plugs and light switches are insulated and protected.

☐ Lights are shielded.

☐ Lighting sufficiently illuminates the gym or wrestling room.

☐ The heating and cooling system for the gym or wrestling room works properly and is monitored regularly.

☐ Ducts, radiators, pipes, and so on are shielded or designed to withstand high impact.

☐ Tamper-free thermostats are housed under impact-resistant covers.

☐ Equipment is inspected before and during each use.

☐ The gym or wrestling room is adequately supervised.

☐ Galleries and viewing areas have been designed to protect small children by blocking their access to the activity area.

☐ The gym or wrestling room (floor, roof, walls, light fixtures, and so on) is inspected annually for safety and structural deficiencies.

☐ Fire alarms are in good working order.

☐ Fire extinguishers are up to date, with a note of last inspection posted.

☐ Directions are posted for evacuation in case of fire.

From ASEP, 2007, *Coaching youth wrestling*, 3rd ed. (Champaign, IL: Human Kinetics).

Informed Consent Form

I hereby give my permission for _____ to participate in _____ during the athletic season beginning on _____. Further, I authorize the school or club to provide emergency treatment of any injury or illness my child may experience if qualified medical personnel consider treatment necessary and perform the treatment. This authorization is granted only if I cannot be reached and reasonable effort has been made to do so.

Parent or guardian: _____

Address: _____

Phone: ( ) _____ **Other phone:** ( ) _____

Additional contact in case of emergency: _____

Relationship to athlete: _____ **Phone:** ( ) _____

Family physician: _____ **Phone:** ( ) _____

Medical conditions (e.g., allergies, chronic illness): _____

_____

_____

_____

_____

My child and I are aware that participating in _____ is a potentially hazardous activity. We assume all risks associated with participation in this sport, including but not limited to falls, contact with other participants, and other reasonable-risk conditions associated with the sport. All such risks to my child are known and appreciated by my child and me.

We understand this informed consent form and agree to its conditions.

Athlete's signature: _____

Date: _____

Parent's or guardian's signature: _____

Date: _____

From ASEP, 2007, *Coaching youth wrestling*, 3rd ed. (Champaign, IL: Human Kinetics).

Injury Report Form

Date of injury: _____ Time: _____ a.m./p.m.
Location: _____

Athlete's name: _____
Age: _____ Date of birth: _____

Type of injury: _____
Anatomical area involved: _____
Cause of injury: _____
_____
_____
_____

Extent of injury: _____
_____
_____
_____

Person administering first aid (name): _____
First aid administered: _____
_____
_____

Other treatment administered: _____
_____
_____

Referral action: _____
_____
_____
_____
_____

Signature of person administering first aid: _____
Date: _____

From ASEP, 2007, *Coaching youth wrestling*, 3rd ed. (Champaign, IL: Human Kinetics).

Emergency Information Card

Athlete's name: _____ Date of birth: _____

Address: _____

Phone: (   ) _____

Provide information for parent or guardian and one additional contact in case of emergency.

Parent's or guardian's name: _____

Address: _____

Phone: (   ) _____ Other phone: (   ) _____

Additional contact's name: _____

Relationship to athlete: _____

Address: _____

Phone: (   ) _____ Other phone: (   ) _____

Insurance Information

Name of insurance company: _____

Policy name and number: _____

Medical Information

Physician's name: _____

Phone: (   ) _____

Is your child allergic to any drugs?   *YES   NO*

If so, what? _____

Does your child have other allergies (e.g., bee stings, dust)? _____

_____

Does your child have any of the following?

asthma   diabetes   epilepsy

Is your child currently taking medication?   *YES   NO*

If so, what? _____

Does your child wear contact lenses?   *YES   NO*

Is there additional information we should know about your child's health or physical condition?   *YES   NO*

If yes, please explain: _____

_____

Parent's or guardian's signature: _____

Date: _____

From ASEP, 2007, *Coaching youth wrestling*, 3rd ed. (Champaign, IL: Human Kinetics).

Emergency Response Card

Be prepared to give the following information to an EMS dispatcher.
(*Note*: Do not hang up first. Let the EMS dispatcher hang up first.)

Caller's name: _____

Telephone number from which the call is being made: _____

Reason for call: _____

How many people are injured: _____

Condition of victim(s): _____

First aid being given: _____

Current location: _____

Address: _____

Directions (e.g., cross streets, landmarks, entrance access):

From ASEP, 2007, *Coaching youth wrestling*, 3rd ed. (Champaign, IL: Human Kinetics).

Appendix B

Wrestling Terms

bottom position—the starting position in which a wrestler's hands are in front of the starting line and the knees behind. The top wrestler assumes the control position by grasping the opponent's near elbow with one hand and the midsection with the other hand. In folkstyle wrestling, a wrestler can choose to start a period from the down position. If action travels out of bounds, the wrestler who is under the control of his or her opponent restarts action from the down position.

breakdown—a technique in folkstyle wrestling in which the wrestler in the top position flattens the bottom wrestler and turns him or her for a pin. Common breakdowns are the tight waist, arm chop, spiral ride, and ankle breakdown.

chicken wing—a common pinning or riding hold. A wrestler chops the opponent's arm and works to overhook the arm. To establish a chicken wing, a wrestler holds an overhook and gets his or her hand across the opponent's back.

choice—in folkstyle wrestling, each wrestler chooses the starting position for one of the periods after the first. Wrestlers start the first period from the neutral position. Before the start of the second period, the referee flips a coin to determine who has first choice for the starting position. The wrestler with the first choice can choose top, bottom, or neutral, or he or she can defer the choice to the third period. As a point of strategy, wrestlers most commonly choose the bottom position because as wrestlers advance in skill, they feel that escapes are easier to achieve.

cradle—a pinning hold that wrestlers learn early in their careers. To gain control of a cradle, a wrestler wraps one arm around the opponent's neck and the other arm around one leg and then locks the hands. The wrestler has "locked up a cradle" and can use it to hold the opponent's shoulders to the mat.

decision—a victory determined by points scored for takedowns, escapes, reversals, near falls, and, in some instances such as college matches, a time advantage.

default—the outcome of a match when one wrestler is injured and unable to wrestle or to continue wrestling.

disqualification—a situation in which a wrestler loses a match because he or she has violated the rules.

escape—getting away from the opponent's control and gaining a neutral position.

fall—the ultimate objective. It occurs when one wrestler pins the opponent's shoulders to the mat for a specified time. The match ends, and the wrestler earning the fall is declared the winner, no matter how many points either wrestler has.

forfeit—the outcome of a match when one wrestler fails to appear.

front headlock—used to counter to an opponent's shot (or attempt at a takedown). The wrestler sprawls the legs back and traps the opponent's head under his or her chest while locking the hands around the neck and one arm. Once a front headlock is controlled, a wrestler will try to go behind the opponent for a takedown.

half nelson—the simplest of the pinning combinations. A wrestler in the top position reaches under an opponent's arm from behind and grabs the back of the opponent's head. He or she then pries the arm up while driving into the opponent until reaching a chest-to-chest position with the arm wrapped around the neck to earn points for a near fall.

illegal hold—a hold or technique that is not allowed. Wrestlers who use an illegal maneuver are penalized one point. Common illegal holds include a full nelson, headlocks in which the wrestler doesn't encircle an arm, or locking hands around an opponent's waist when the wrestler is on top or in control of the opponent on the mat.

intentional release—a tactic used by a wrestler who is skilled at takedowns or who needs to catch up in points. The controlling wrestler intentionally releases the opponent, allowing an escape point to the opponent. The wrestler then tries to score a takedown for two points, thus trading the opponent's one point for the release for a takedown that is worth two points. This tactic is also known as *cutting him (or her)*.

leg ride—a technique in which the wrestler in the top position uses the legs to turn an opponent. This is also called the grapevine position. A leg ride also is an effective way to ride out an opponent (*see also* entry for *ride*).

major decision—the situation in folkstyle wrestling in which a wrestler wins a match by 8 to 14 points.

near fall—the situation in which a wrestler's shoulders are held in the danger, or exposed, position: one shoulder on the mat and the other within 45 degrees of the mat. Near fall points are also known as back points. Once a wrestler's shoulders break a 45-degree angle with the mat, the referee begins to count. If the shoulders are exposed for two seconds, the opponent earns two points. Five seconds are worth three points.

pin—synonymous with fall.

reversal—exchanging control from the bottom to the top position.

ride—the position of the wrestler on top who is working for a breakdown and turn to a pin. Wrestlers also ride out an opponent late in a match when they are ahead to prevent the opponent from getting an escape or reversal for one or two points.

scramble—a wild flurry of action that occurs when neither wrestler has control over the other or when one has tenuous control. A good scrambler uses any legal means necessary to stop a takedown attempt and convert it to his or her own score. Scrambling rarely consists of sound basic techniques.

setup—strategies used to maneuver an opponent out of position so that the wrestler can initiate a score. From the neutral position, a wrestler might set up the opponent by popping the opponent's arms up or dragging them across his or her body.

shoot—to attack and work for a takedown. The technique is known as a shot. A wrestler shoots on the opponent in a variety of ways with different takedowns, such as single leg, high-crotch, or low single.

sprawl—to throw the legs back to counter a shot or an attack. From a sprawl, wrestlers learn counterattacks such as snapping and spinning behind or locking up a front headlock.

stalling—trying to slow the pace of the match, also referred to as passivity. This may happen when a wrestler is tired or is trying to protect a lead. The referee can warn a wrestler for stalling. A second stalling call earns the opponent a point.

stance—the starting position of the wrestler. In a square stance, the wrestler's feet are wide below the shoulders. In a staggered stance, one foot is forward in a stride position.

stand-up—a technique used to escape from an opponent. The wrestler must clear his or her arms and step up while pressing back into the top wrestler. Once the wrestler is on the feet, he or she must maintain balance and peel the opponent's hands off to break the lock and turn to face the opponent. All of this happens while the top wrestler aggressively works to return the opponent to the mat.

switch—commonly the first reversal technique taught to wrestlers. A switch involves clearing the arms, sitting to a hip, reaching back to the inside of the opponent's thigh, and using leverage to turn and complete a reversal. From the bottom position, wrestlers can score by escaping their opponent's grasp (worth one point) or reversing their opponent's control (worth two points).

takedown—a maneuver to establish control from an open position in which neither wrestler has control. A takedown is worth two points in folkstyle wrestling. In freestyle and Greco-Roman wrestling, a takedown may be worth one, two, three, or five points, depending on the amplitude of the takedown.

technical fall—the situation in which a wrestler is declared the winner of a match by reaching a particular point spread.

throw—quickly forcing an opponent from the feet to his or her back. Common throws include the headlock and reverse headlock.

tie-up—wrestlers' contact with each other from the neutral position. Common tie-ups include underhooks, overhooks, and head ties.

turn—to force an opponent into a near fall position.

whizzer—a technique in which a wrestler wraps his or her arm over the opponent's arm when it is around the body or leg and uses it to develop leverage to counter an attack.

Appendix C

23 Wrestling Activities

In this appendix, you will find 23 activities to use in your wrestling program. Use these wrestling activities during practices to help keep motivation and interest high and to keep the sport fun.

Switcher

Goal

To gain control of an opponent.

Description

Pair the wrestlers and have them get down on all fours, side by side, facing each other's ankles. With the inside arm, each wrestler reaches inside the nearest thigh. Neither wrestler has an advantage. On the signal, each wrestler attempts to gain control over the opponent.

Wrestlers should work to drive into the other wrestler, use the leg for leverage, try to get into switch or hip-heist position, keep the opponent from driving them to a hip, and ultimately to gain control. This is a classic scramble situation.

Variations

- One wrestler is seated on the mat. The other is alongside in the basic bottom starting position, facing the opposite direction with his or her near arm across the seated wrestler's waist. When ready, the seated wrestler uses his or her near arm to reach over the opponent's near arm and inside the opponent's near leg, in the switch position. On the signal, the seated wrestler tries to complete the switch. The other will resist the switch until it is inevitable, then as the switcher comes on top into a riding position, the wrestler will start his or her own reswitch.
- Have the wrestlers do the variation with low resistance so they can learn to feel when the reswitch is available to them.

Wrestler's Handshake

Goal

To learn motion in a stance with contact.

Description

Pair the wrestlers and have them get in their strong neutral-position stance and grab each other at the forearm, right arm to right arm, or left to left. On the signal, the wrestlers should use proper motion in their stance and proper forearm control so that their free arms can reach behind the opponent to grab the far hip. The wrestlers work to get behind the opponent so they can lift and bring the opponent to the mat for a takedown.

Variation

- Have one wrestler grab the opponent's wrist—right to right, or left to left. Then he or she uses the free hand to grab that arm above the elbow. On the signal, the attacker uses motion, stance, and the tie-up to try to reach behind and grab the far hip as described earlier. This leads into the two-on-one (or "Russian tie") as the wrestlers advance.

Caged-Up

Goal

To learn to move and fight through contact.

Description

Divide wrestlers into groups of six. Five wrestlers stand hip to hip in a circle with their hands around one another's backs to form a "cage" around one wrestler. The wrestlers can shift left and right with the hips and legs to move the cage, but the wrestlers' feet must stay planted on the ground and they must keep their arms intertwined. On the signal, the wrestler inside the cage must use good stance and motion to fight through the gaps of the cage to get out.

Variations

- If the cage is too difficult to overcome, have the wrestlers forming the cage spread their feet more widely.
- Use time limits and encouragement or change the cage tactics to prevent young wrestlers from becoming humiliated in this setting.

Coiled Spring

Goal

To help the attacker learn the correct way to take an opponent down with a single leg and to teach the defender how to go to the mat when the takedown is inevitable.

Description

Pair the wrestlers. One is the attacker and one is the defender. Using a single-leg attack, the attacker takes control of one of the defender's legs and maintains a stance with the head up and in the defender's chest. On the signal, the attacker changes levels and attempts to drive the defender to the mat with a single-leg takedown. At the same time, the defender works to maintain balance and return quickly to a safe position when necessary. Once the defender falls to the mat, the attacker continues to control the single leg and maintain balance while standing over the defender. When the takedown is inevitable, the defender works to avoid going down to his or her back, potentially giving up near fall points. The defender should work to go down in a strong position and then get to the base position as quickly as possible so that he or she can use this strong coiled position to quickly spring to the feet with a stand-up.

Variations

- Perform this drill using a time limit or as a race against another pair of wrestlers.
- Teach the defender to fall to the belly so that he or she is not overpowered on a takedown, and keep track of the number of times the defender does this.

Bull Riding

Goal

To practice movement in the bottom position.

Description

Pair the wrestlers. One wrestler, the bull, assumes the bottom starting position. The other wrestler, the cowboy, sits on the bottom wrestler's back, near the hips, with the feet off the floor. The cowboy can try to hang on to the bull but cannot lock hands or grasp the clothing. On the signal, the bottom wrestler changes direction by crawling forward or backward or spinning while keeping the hands and knees on the mat. The other wrestler must attempt to ride the bull for at least 8 seconds without putting his or her feet down or falling off.

Variations

- Award the cowboy one point for a successful ride, and award the bull one point for knocking the cowboy off. Play against other pairs of wrestlers.
- Allow the cowboy to put his or her feet on the ground.
- Do not allow the cowboy to hold on to the bull with the hands and arms.
- Allow the bull to buck by rising up off the knees while keeping the hands and feet on the mat.

Fox Tail

Goal

To practice movement in the neutral position.

Description

Pair the wrestlers and give each one a sock or short towel to tuck into the back of his or her shorts, leaving four to six inches out to form a tail. On the signal, the wrestlers attempt to pull their partner's tail out.

Variations

- Award one point each time a wrestler pulls a tail. Play against other pairs of wrestlers.
- Lengthen or shorten the tail.
- Allow wrestlers to use only one hand.

Spinning Bear

Goal

To give the defender experience facing an opponent on the mat while the attacker works to score a takedown by getting behind the defender.

Description

Pair the wrestlers. The defender is in a bear crawl position with only the hands and feet on the mat. The attacker is in a good stance on his or her feet, facing the defender, with his or her hands on the defender's shoulders. On the signal, the attacker attempts to spin behind the bear, keeping the hands on the bear at all times. The bear cannot grab the attacker or drop to the knees, but, rather, the bear should keep the head up and move the feet and hands in an attempt keep the attacker in front as long as possible.

Variation

- Require that the bear give up control of one arm to the opponent to start.

Crack the Whip

Goal

To teach wrestlers how to scramble and return to a correct stance.

Description

Pair the wrestlers. The defender is on the mat in a position similar to the bottom starting position except that the other wrestler, the attacker, is standing behind, grasping one of the defender's ankles and holding it high against his or her body. The attacker should be in a strong takedown stance while holding the defender's ankle tightly with only the hands, relatively high toward the chest. On the signal, the defender attempts to "crack the whip" and escape the ankle control of the attacking wrestler and return to a neutral stance. The bottom wrestler can do things such as push back then quickly drive forward and try to rapidly back into the attacker to put weight over the ankle.

Variations

- Give the attacker more control farther up the defender's leg.
- Have the attacker start by grasping the ankle while the defender is in the full bottom starting position.

Bone Fight

Goal

To practice changing levels and moving.

Description

Pair the wrestlers and give each pair a towel. Each wrestler holds one end of the towel with one hand without wrapping it around the hand. The wrestlers must stay in a solid stance on their feet. On the signal, the wrestlers attempt to break each other's grip on the towel or to knock each other off balance by moving in their stance, by changing levels, and by pulling with the towel grip. Award one point each time a wrestler breaks the opponent's grip.

Variations

- Award a point each time any part of the opponent's body, other than the feet, touches the floor.
- Shorten or lengthen the towel.
- Award a point to the other wrestler any time a wrestler comes out of his or her stance.

Face-Off

Goal

To learn the hip movement from the bottom position.

Description

Pair the wrestlers. The bottom wrestler kneels with the hands on the mat at his or her sides. The top wrestler kneels behind the bottom wrestler, underhooking both of the bottom wrestler's arms from behind without locking the hands. On the signal, the bottom wrestler battles away from the arms and faces the top wrestler, while the top wrestler attempts to drive the bottom wrestler to the belly and hold him or her there.

Variations

- The bottom wrestler starts in the bottom starting position with the top wrestler's chest lightly on his or her back, underhooking both of the bottom wrestler's arms.
- The bottom wrestler starts from a seated position on the mat, legs straight out in front. The top wrestler is seated directly behind, chest to back, with underhooks on both sides.

Flopping Fish

Goal

To learn ways to pin a defender for the fall.

Description

Pair the wrestlers and have them lie side by side on their backs, head to head and feet to feet, with their legs straight and their arms and hands along their sides on the mat. On the signal, the wrestlers work to control the other person and hold them on their back in a near fall situation. Award two points when a wrestler holds the other wrestler for 5 seconds and award three points when a wrestler holds the opponent for 10 seconds.

Variation

- Allow one or both wrestlers to start with legs bent or the inside arm across the other wrestler's chest.

Cricket and Wicket

Goal

To initiate proper level change and penetration.

Description

Pair the wrestlers and have them assume their strong neutral-position stance. On the signal, one wrestler makes a deep level change and penetrates all the way between and through the stationary partner's legs. After the shot, the stationary wrestler leans over and places his or her hands on the knees and ducks the head. The shooter turns around and leaps back over the partner in a leapfrog motion, then spins back to his or her stance to prepare for the next repetition.

Variations

- To make this easier, have the stationary wrestler place his or her hands on the mat after the shot.
- Increase the pace of this activity for wrestlers with greater physical ability.

Knee Tag

Goal

To work on changing levels and penetrating.

Description

Pair the wrestlers and have them assume their strong neutral-position stance. On the signal, they move and change levels to attempt to tag the inside of their partner's knee with their hand.

Variations

- One wrestler tags and the other defends without using hands.
- Award points for tags to the inside of the knee.

Sneaky Snap

Goal

To practice moving an opponent with a head tie.

Description

Pair the wrestlers. Both wrestlers are on their feet in their strong stance. One wrestler is the attacker and controls a collar tie—one hand on the neck, the other on the opposite arm—on the other wrestler, who is the defender.

On the signal, the attacker uses motion and level changes to circle and move the defender by controlling the head. If the attacker gets a snap-down by changing levels and taking the head to the mat and is able to get behind the defender for a takedown, award two points. If the defender creates an angle for a successful single- or double-leg takedown, award one point. The defender cannot use his or her hands for balance or to shoot on the attacker.

Variations

- To make this easier, have the defender keep the hands down.
- To make this more challenging, set a time limit.

Whizzer

Goal

To control an opponent's motion.

Description

Pair the wrestlers and have both assume a strong bottom starting position, side by side and facing the same direction in the center of the 10-foot circle. One wrestler places an arm across the other's back. The other wrestler locks a whizzer by driving his or her arm over the other's arm and between their bodies. On the signal, the wrestlers attempt to drive their opponent out of bounds or throw them to their back. When young wrestlers face a whizzer, they are often tempted to step over their opponent. This can cause them to fall onto their back. Therefore, coach them to do this drill without stepping over their opponent's body.

Variation

- Have each wrestler start his or her turn with the head on the mat (the wrestler whose head and chest is higher is in the dominant position). The wrestler with the high head will have an easier time, and the one with the head down will have a more difficult time.

Rescue Mission

Goal

To practice lifting.

Description

Divide wrestlers into groups of four. Three wrestlers are on one side of the mat, and one wrestler is on the other. The single wrestler acts as the rescuer, and on the signal, runs across the mat, lifts one of the teammates, and carries the teammate back across the mat. He or she then runs back and does the same for each of the remaining teammates. The first team to move all three wrestlers across the mat scores a point. Switch wrestlers until everyone has had a turn as the rescuer.

Variations

- Decrease the distance for the carry, or allow the rescuer to drag the teammates only halfway.
- Require teammates to play dead and remain limp during the lift and carry.

Log Lift

Goal

To learn proper lifting technique with an emphasis on leg and hip power.

Description

Pair the wrestlers and have them lock into a reverse lift position around their opponent's body. To get into the lock, each participant must step the right leg to the inside of the other's right leg and then lean forward and lock the hands just above the opponent's waist, facing away from the other wrestler's head. On the signal, each wrestler attempts to lift the opponent off the ground without tripping him or her.

Variations

- For less experienced wrestlers, have one wrestler bend at the waist and place his or her hands on the knees. The other wrestler gets the lock around the waist, steps the leg inside the other's leg (left inside left, or right inside right), drives the hips in, and lifts the wrestler off the mat.
- To make this a bit more difficult, have one wrestler get into the bottom starting position and then go through the movement.

Stuck in the Mud

Goal

To enhance the attacker's ability to score takedowns and the defender's ability to defend against leg attacks.

Description

Pair the wrestlers. The defender kneels on the left leg, with the right foot on the mat far in front of the knee. The attacker wraps the right arm, armpit deep, above the shoelaces of the kneeling wrestler. On the signal, the defender sits back on the attacker's shoulders and attempts to keep weight on the attacker to keep him or her from gaining control of the far leg.

Variation

- Allow the attacker to stand up with the defender's leg and trip the defender to the mat.

Turk Step Chase

Goal

To practice scoring near fall points.

Description

Pair the wrestlers. The defender lies facedown with legs straight. The other wrestler is on top of the bottom wrestler with one leg between the defender's legs. On the signal, the defender attempts to crawl to a target (e.g., out of a circle or to the edge of the mat) by pulling himself or herself along with only the elbows and forearms and without using the legs. At the same time, the attacker attempts to prevent the defender from reaching the target by using a turk step to turn the defender over and secure one of the legs with both of his or her own.

Variation

- Have the top wrestler get a leg inside and under the bottom wrestler's near leg above the knee before starting. This makes it easier for the top wrestler and more difficult for the bottom wrestler.

Switcheroo

Goal

To work on the back step and lifting.

Description

Pair the wrestlers and have them lock their arms over and under each other, while standing chest to chest. On the signal, each wrestler tries to knock the opponent to the ground without breaking the grip. Award one point for each knockdown.

Variations

- Have the partners lock only the arms.
- Don't allow tripping.

Toe Tackle

Goal

To initiate a takedown.

Description

Pair the wrestlers and have them grasp their opponent's shoulders. They should be approximately an arm's length from each other. On the signal, the wrestlers attempt a takedown by using their legs and feet to trip their opponent. Wrestlers may not move or pummel for position with their hands nor shoot or snap down the opponent. Award one point for a successful trip.

Variation

- To increase the contact, let the wrestlers start chest to chest in an over-under position—each with one arm in an overhook and the other in an underhook, also known as the pummeling position.

Spider Fight

Goal

To practice the back arch.

Description

Pair the wrestlers. With the wrestlers facing away from each other, have them assume a back-arch position by arching the belly toward the ceiling so that the head hangs upside down and only the hands and feet touch the mat ("the spider position"). On the signal, each wrestler attempts to knock the opponent out of this position by grabbing, pulling, or pushing. Award one point for each knockdown.

Variations

- Have wrestlers use a crab position. Starting from a sitting position with the legs in front, wrestlers push the hips up so that only the hands and feet are on the mat.
- Allow the wrestlers to use only their left hands to fight.

Pummeling Around

Goal

To increase activity and awareness from a close pummeling situation.

Description

Pair the wrestlers and have them stand chest to chest, in an over-under position. On the signal, the wrestlers attempt to lift and throw their opponent to their back using underhook and overhook control. Mastering these moves provides the foundation for learning the back arch and back step.

Variations

- As the wrestlers advance, have them incorporate actual pummeling— release the overhook and try to drive that hand and arm between the two bodies so that it can come back up into an underhook. Repeat the drill as each wrestler finds himself or herself in a new overhook.
- While pummeling is underway, on your signal, have both wrestlers seek inside control and lift and throw their opponent.

About ASEP

Coaching Youth Wrestling was written by the American Sport Education Program (ASEP) in conjunction with USA Wrestling. ASEP has been developing and delivering coaching education courses since 1981. As the nation's leading coaching education program, ASEP works with national, state, and local youth sport organizations to develop educational programs for coaches, officials, administrators, and parents. These programs incorporate ASEP's philosophy of "Athletes first, winning second."

USA Wrestling is the national governing body for the sport of wrestling in the United States and the central organization for the coordination and support of amateur wrestling programs in the nation. USA Wrestling works to increase appreciation for and participation in the international styles of wrestling (freestyle and Greco-Roman) as well as folk-style wrestling. USA Wrestling has more than 159,000 members, including athletes of all ages, coaches, officials, and parents.

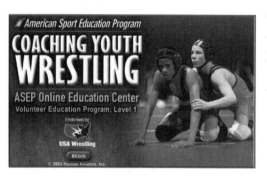

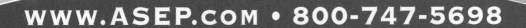